Getting Straight 'A's

Competition for entry to top universities has never been stiffer. As a result, if you are to secure a place on the course of your choice then top grades are absolutely essential. *Getting Straight 'A's* is packed full of invaluable advice that will help you to maximise your academic potential and achieve the results you need.

Written by an acknowledged expert in the field, this study guide will help you to:

- assess your own strengths and weaknesses;
- make best use of the resources available to you;
- effectively manage your time and prioritise your workload;
- develop essay-writing and note-taking skills;
- excel in exams and coursework.

Complete with self-assessment exercises to help you to hone your study and exam skills, this book is designed to help high-flyers who are both ambitious and aware of their talent. The perfect companion to the same author's book *Studying for Success*, this book will help those who aim for the top to reach it!

Richard Palmer is Head of English at Bedford School. His other Routledge titles include *The Good Grammar Guide* and *Write in Style*.

Getting Straight 'A's
A students' guide to success

Richard Palmer

Routledge
Taylor & Francis Group

LONDON AND NEW YORK

First published 2006

By Routledge
2 Park Square, Milton Park,
Abingdon, Oxon OX14 4RN

Simultaneously published in the USA and Canada
By Routledge
270 Madison Ave, New York, NY 10016

Routledge is an imprint of the Taylor & Francis Group

© 2006 Richard Palmer

Typset in Sabon by
Florence Production Ltd, Stoodleigh, Devon
Printed and bound in Great Britain by
TJ International Ltd, Padstow, Cornwall

British Library Cataloguing in Publication Data
A catalogue record for this book is available from the British
Library

Library of Congress Cataloging in Publication Data
Palmer, Richard, 1947–
    Getting straight 'A's: a students' guide to success/
Richard Palmer.
        p. cm
    Included bibliographical references and index
    Academic achievement.   I, Title.
    LB1049.P353 2005
    371.3′028′1 – sdc22   2005006980

ISBN 0–415–35623–7

This book is dedicated to the Class of 2003–5, International Baccalaureate Higher Level English A1, Bedford School:

Alex Burt, Tom Day, Sebastian Del Monte, Jaron Dosanjh, Tom Howell, Mark Papworth, John Richter and Will Young.

The best set I have encountered in 35 years; I hope I taught them as much and as well as they taught me.

Contents

Preface and acknowledgements

Of all the rewards and satisfactions that can come a teacher's way, the greatest – well, for this one anyway – is in encountering really bright pupils who push you as much as you push them. It is no less stimulating to cater for such students as an author, and writing this book – aimed as its title indicates at students both gifted and hungry to learn – has been a genuine pleasure. And a key factor in that enjoyment has been the freedom to be *tough*. I hope you will find what follows entertaining, enabling and encouraging; however, there are times when I pour scorn on certain 'Study Skills' myths and techniques, and also occasions when my advice to you will seem brusque (though I hope never unsympathetic). And in that tough vein, here for a start are seven things which this book will not or cannot do:

- provide you with a brain transplant;
- offer any smart-alec tips on how to 'beat the system';
- reduce your responsibility for your own work;
- transform all your work-time into unmitigated joy;
- turn you into an automatic expert in all the subjects you are studying and on which you will be examined;
- add anything significant to your *subject-knowledge*.

And perhaps most important of all:

- make you 'care'.

Those 'early warnings' are important, but you are probably already aware of the dangers or futilities they address. For as should be evident, I am assuming that you are talented, committed and used to success. All those are of course major pluses; however, ambitious students – and some of the adults who advise them – sometimes make mistakes in their approach or how they deploy their time. They may not be as obviously 'wrong' as the notions just listed, but they can still be damaging. Chief among them is the idea that 'effort' is not only its own reward but a kind of elixir that will guarantee triumph. On the contrary:

- you can't do it all through sheer slog. Indeed . . .
- . . . you can work *too* hard, to the detriment of success.

On more than one occasion I shall be talking about the difference between working *hard* and working *well*, and it would be sensible to get that distinction into your mindset as soon as you can.

Next, and more affirmatively, two things to which some bright students of my acquaintance do not pay enough attention:

- organisation is paramount
- learn from everyone and everything.

Truly successful students:

1   know their own work-rhythms and act on them;
2   are 'in charge' of their equipment, books and materials;
3   manage their time well and are never ambushed by deadlines;
4   rarely if ever need to do assignments at the last moment;
5   regard learning as an open-ended process that transcends subject-barriers or syllabuses;
6   are genuine thinkers.

That last item brings me to what in some ways is the heart of this book.

Getting Straight 'A's is the fourth 'Study Skills' title I have published, but in truth I have come to detest that phrase. The fact that it has become a trendy cure-all is bad enough; worse is its fundamental vagueness. A much better, though less suave/PR-adaptable term, is 'Techniques for Learning', which is preferable for one overwhelming reason:

It puts the emphasis on what you *know* rather than the much less precise concept of what, in certain circumstances, you *can or might be able to <u>do</u>* i.e. skills.

The focus on *'knowledge'* takes in something that a concern with mere *'skills'* can never do – alerting ourselves to what we cannot or do not know.

Skills is actually a very precarious concept. It seems to embody, or at least imply, the notion that anyone can acquire them. That may be true up to a point; what emphatically is *not* true is that the acquisition of such skills automatically makes you a good thinker, a good student, a good professional. In the end, 'skills' are like Boy Scout Merit badges: they don't tell anyone – including you – very much about you. But someone who knows *how to think* – which includes the ability to identify wrong thinking, cosy thinking, lazy thinking or stuff that is just rubbish – is a much rarer being, and also a more interesting and successful one.

That's why I have devoted Chapter 4 to *Thinking For Fun and Profit*, which is designed to sharpen your thinking processes and make you critically aware of the whole business of arguing. It is quite unlike anything I wrote in those previous books; more than any other chapter it is aimed at the gifted and talented as a decisive aid to acquiring the clarity of mind that characterises all work of distinction. It might seem to be aimed chiefly at 'Advanced' (16+) students, but younger ones among you may also find it of interest and use, since much of the material and the issues it embraces will soon impinge on you.

In that chapter I draw on *Theory of Knowledge* by Nicholas Alchin and the teaching of IBO consultant Richard van de Lagemaat; I am grateful for all that they provided and inspired; I also learned much from the work of a fellow Routledge author, John Kirkman. It is a pleasure to acknowledge the ideas and wisdom of many colleagues past and present (particularly Colin Baker, Jenny Gillett, Colin Marsh and Philip Young) and nearly all my students too, not just those named in the Dedication. I am no less grateful to my Editor, Philip Mudd, who commissioned the book in the first place and has been an indispensable guide throughout. Finally and as always, I thank my wife Ann for all she is and does, not least putting up with the hours I spend chained to my PC.

Richard Palmer
Bedford, February 2005

Chapter 1

Naming it

Preliminary: why real achievers don't do drugs

The drugs in question are nothing to do with those that are smoked, sniffed, swallowed or syringed. I have in mind a quite different kind of Class A Substance Abuse; curiously enough, they too all begin with 'S':

1   superstition
2   self-delusion
3   showmanship
4   smart-alec ruses
5   study aids
6   surfing the Net.

The last two are fairly recent comers to the party; the others have been around almost as long as humankind itself. All six are deadly enemies to the would-be high-flyer.

- If you imagine that your chances of succeeding in an exam hinge on whether or not you 'have a good day' or on whom your examiner might be, you are being both 'superstitious' and 'self-deluded', and that will cost you dearly unless you change your thinking.
- If you think that impressing a marker or an examiner is a matter of flashy presentation or clever-clever 'performance art', you are again deluding yourself and also adopting the mindset of the 'smart-alec'; that too will cost you dearly.
- And if you believe that 'Study Aids' and a 'plethora of websites' will guarantee you high success, you are playing an

extremely dangerous game that might result in losing everything you're going for. First, you are substituting secondary sources for irreplaceable primary ones – your syllabuses, your texts, your teachers and above all your own brain. Second, a great number of such Aids, either in pulped-tree or electronic form, are mediocre; many are distinctly poor; some are almost indescribably bad.

Those six 'drugs' are bad news in and of themselves. Moreover, just as much as physical narcotics, they erode, often rapidly, your most priceless asset:

You.

The motto 'I am in charge' should be adopted by all high-flyers. If you think exams are a lottery and examiners stupid, gullible or hostile, *you are not in charge*. If you think snazzy fonts, beautifully manicured handwriting and other forms of surface charm are more important than substance, *you are not in charge*. If you mortgage your brain to the whims of this Study Aid hack or that Internet clown, *you are not in charge*.

I shall return to all these issues later in the chapter. But first I want to banish the impression those stern paragraphs may have given that I am unsympathetic to students or unaware of the reasons why they feel tempted to 'do drugs' in the way I've outlined. On the contrary, students of all kinds have my profound and in many respects enraged sympathy.

Situation report

On one level, this can be summarised very succinctly.

There has probably never been a more difficult time to be a student than the early twenty-first century.

Money

Gone are the days when the state funded undergraduates in the belief that investing in such talent had great social potential as well as being worth doing for its own sake. *Student grants* belong to ancient history, replaced by *loans* which, while administered in a flexible and friendly way, still cast a long shadow over a student's future. There's also the matter of fees as well as living expenses – another major change from my own day or indeed ten years ago.

Expectations (1)

Here are three possible answers to the question, 'Why are you doing your course?':

		✓
A	Because you love it	
B	Because it's important in advancement/career terms	
C	Because you've got nothing else to do	

Option C might look like a joke but it is not intended as one. The pressure on young people to continue their studies is huge; as a result the alternatives are fewer in number and less attractive than used to pertain. At present, the UK's undergraduate population comprises just over 30 per cent of the 18–22 age-group. A generation ago the figure was less than 10 per cent; in a generation's time – if the Prime Minister at the time of writing has his way – it will reach 50 per cent.[1] More and more young people are going to find that little else is available other than tertiary education; in addition, the social and parental pressure on them to 'conform' to this grand plan will be enormous.

Now, all that may not seem much of a dilemma or cause for concern to a high-flyer of 16+ already armed with a fistful of Grade As and A*s or one about to become such. However, it is intrinsic to the educational culture you inhabit, and it may affect you more than you think, especially if you don't take steps to ensure that your study is pleasurable as well as necessary. Naturally, this book is devoted to helping you achieve that, but the process needs to start in your own mind.

Expectations (2)

Not only are more and more young people forcibly encouraged to remain as students: they are expected to perform better than their predecessors. Every summer, when results at all levels are published, the media mainlines on whether there has been a percentile improvement on last year overall. Well, that's not quite true: *there is _always_ such a rise*.[2] What exercises correspondents, pundits and indeed students themselves is *how much* of an 'improvement' there has been, whether there are any maverick subjects which have dipped, and of course what the various league tables supposedly demonstrate about the state of our schools, colleges and universities.

It would be easy to blame the media for this performance-grade obsession and the accompanying impression that education is solely about successful 'product'. I am not going to do that, on the grounds that it would be not unlike blaming a bomb for going off rather than censuring whoever placed, threw or indeed manufactured it. Such reporting merely reflects the values and obsessions of educational systems themselves – and if you thought the analogy I've just offered was aggressive, that is entirely apposite. It would not quite be fair to suggest that those systems 'are out to get you', but they are not interested in the benefit of the doubt or in anything that cannot be visibly proved. That has major implications for you.

Assessment-driven curricula: the dangers and the price

The overwhelming majority of Western curricula (certainly all those currently operational in the UK[3]) are based on *performance* rather than *learning*. Some might say that is a false distinction, even a silly one: to perform well must, presumably, depend on a solid learning base. Well, yes – but also *no*. If you insist that all programmes of academic study are to be assessment-driven, a number of things happen, all of them regrettable or worse.

• An ethos arises where students think – sometimes are *taught* – that it's more important to know the answer than value the question for its own sake and for everything that stems from it. Those things may not impinge on the 'answer', but they are of enriching and often decisive significance – sometimes more so than the answer itself. To bypass that is to champion product at the direct expense of 'process'.

- Assessment-driven curricula invariably prevent pupils from doing things they like and are interested in, not least because their teachers are prevented from discovering what those things are and acting accordingly; sometimes *the pupils themselves* never discover those enthusiasms until much later. It hardly needs saying that the educational consequences here are highly damaging however impressive the 'results' can be made to look. Another example of process being ignored in the interests of product.

- Assessment-driven curricula are without exception conservative, cautious, even fearful. Their chief criterion is not to stimulate but to avoid controversy and offence. That, to put it mildly, is unfortunate. Just as if you decide to ban any joke that might offend someone, somewhere, you in effect ban all jokes, so if you avoid setting exam tasks which might possibly offend somebody out there, then you can't set anything which will interest pupils (especially the brighter ones).

- If UK GCSE is any guide, assessment-driven curricula are also astoundingly repetitive. It has recently been estimated that across a nine-subject programme, pupils will perform the task of 'analytical critical review' no less than *thirty-four* times! No wonder many students tend to find such a programme not only tedious but an exercise in 'ticking off requirements' which has little to do with any penetrating enquiry.

- Finally, despite some significant attempts to stem it, this tide seems to be swelling. Many pupils are asked to sit tests at what strikes many teachers – and parents – as an absurdly young age. Furthermore, all younger children are spending more time than ever before on preparing themselves for such testing – which must mean that they have less time to *learn*. Higher up the age range, league tables are more complex and domineering than ever. And coursework – the one area where an enterprising student can show true initiative and challenging independence of thought – is under increasing attack because (some say) it encourages plagiarism and/or other forms of cheating.

All that makes pretty grim reading for my target audience, doesn't it? If student assessment is centrally a matter of box-ticking, politically correct blandness and generally 'being a good boy or girl', where does that leave ambitious high-flyers looking for both signal success and the belief that such success actually means something? Is there any *good* news for you?

Yes, lots – otherwise I wouldn't have written this book. To begin with, I am sufficiently idealistic *and* realistic to believe that the hunger to learn as well as succeed will never be vanquished by even the most totalitarian systems of education.[4] Soon we shall be investigating ways in which you can look to make your work an enjoyable, playful, even enticing activity. But first, a wonderful paradox:

> **Nearly everything I have outlined as a problem or disadvantage to high-flyers can be put to their 'success-guaranteed' profit.**

My concerns and objections above are philosophically educational ones, and I hope that as bright young people you share them, or at least recognise their validity. On the other hand, if the emphasis is so predominantly on product and assessed results, that in a way makes it easier for you. You are not going to be asked to do anything that challenges your intellect or stretches your imagination, you will not encounter 'trick' questions,[5] and you certainly will not need to be original. For the student chasing 'Straight "A"s' the key qualities for assignments and exams are

Clarity   Efficiency   Relevance

It would be simplistic to suggest that:

> **All that will be required of you is to do what you're told when you're told to do it.**

but the formula is worth bearing in mind during an exam, and it will do you no harm in other contexts too.

Nevertheless, it won't give you much 'fun', 'pleasure' or 'excitement' – things which bright students need to perform at their best even if (another paradox, and a worrying one) those who design and run our curricula seem oblivious of the notion. And although you will do very well if you 'take care of business' in the way I've been outlining, you'll do even better if you have a good time while doing it.

The importance of the pleasure principle

It is a fact of life that these three things go together:

Enjoyment → Confidence → Success

The formula holds true for almost any activity one could name. Assuming that you have some aptitude, once you acquire one of them, the others follow, often rapidly. Conversely, once you lose any of them, the others tend to fade as well. And since they *are* so intimately connected, it might seem odd to single out one as more fundamental than the others. But for high-flying students, I believe 'enjoyment' is the key. It is also a more complex concept than might first appear.

The student has not yet been born who is capable of enjoying all his/her work all the time. In any course of study there are going to be boring, difficult or even enraging bits which have to be ground through with gritted teeth. That is perfectly normal and perfectly all right: again, it is true of anything in life. But it does mean that we need to extend the meaning of enjoyment to something beyond just *pleasure*, important though the latter is.

In most Western countries or those which follow a broadly Western educational system, students study a large number of subjects until their mid-to-late teens, and then specialise to a greater or lesser extent. In the UK that 'cut-off point' currently occurs at 16+, and one of the questions I regularly ask my own students as they near that momentous stage is:

How many of you are looking forward to giving up at least one subject?

A forest of hands goes up at this, an almost unanimous count. Hardly less populous is the response to my follow-up question:

How many of you are looking forward to giving up *several* subjects?

I then say to them:

When the results come out in the late summer, I *guarantee* that many of you will have secured an

A or even A* grade in a subject you've just told me you detest, and quite a number of you will have several such successes.

I'm talking about bright-to-very-bright students; but then I'm talking *to* them as well: you. And to return to that consideration of enjoyment, it is possible for the bright student to derive a lot of satisfaction out of 'defeating' something, especially a subject s/he does not find congenial.

Enjoyment can mean *victory* as well as *pleasure*. That can even include *revenge* – the enormously satisfying experience of showing those who doubted you (including, perhaps, you yourself) that they were mistaken.

Enjoyment, then, does not just consist of private pleasure, that lovely feeling of doing something well for its own sake and even being lost in the activity because you like it so much. It also incorporates an awareness – both determined and serene – of the public rewards that will eventually come your way. It additionally signifies a 'feel-good factor' that is entirely admirable for all its apparent conceit – the sheer satisfaction one derives from simply being good at something. Anyone with a particular set of skills enjoys using them, and that is as true for students as for anyone else. And if you think I'm encouraging you to cultivate a degree of vanity, you are spot on (see Chapter 2). Nobody ever did anything worthwhile through believing they were other than good at it; that is what 'confidence' means.

The bulk of this book investigates further ways in which you can harness that sense of enjoyment and confidence to ensure 'success' at the highest level. And with the same ends in mind, the rest of this chapter returns us to our beginning.

Seductive stupidities: those 'S' words revisited

We are all to some degree prone to superstition. Rare, if not unique, is the person who has not spoken of 'fingers crossed' or 'touching wood',[6] declared 'third time lucky' or cited 'Friday the thirteenth' as a reason for things having gone badly. That may be harmless drivel, but drivel it is; and it becomes anything *but* harmless when otherwise sentient people organise their lives according to whether Uranus is in the House of Saturn or any other astrological nonsense. The great Richard Dawkins has argued that:

If astrologers cannot be sued by individuals misadvised, say, into taking disastrous business decisions, why at least are they not prosecuted for false representations under the Trade Descriptions Act and driven out of business? Why, actually, are professional astrologers not jailed for fraud?[7]

It is hard to see that last coming about, but that doesn't stop me agreeing with him in full.

I'm not indulging in scabrous prejudice but making a point fundamental to the fortunes of all ambitious people, students or otherwise. The capacity to succeed lies primarily in *you*. Other factors, such as the quality of your teachers and fellow-students, the resources at your disposal, even the occasional stroke of luck,[8] may play their part, but you are by a mile the main actor.

If things go well, that is to your credit; if things do not, that is your fault.

That's a summary as tough as it is bald, and on occasion it won't be quite fair – either way. But I am convinced it is largely true, and I'm comforted to know that William Shakespeare was regularly of the same view. In *Julius Caesar*, Cassius observes:

The fault . . . lies not in our stars but in ourselves.

Right. And so is Edmund in *King Lear*, commenting witheringly on his father's belief that what we human beings are like or get up to is determined by galactic objects light years away:

when we are sick in fortune, often the surfeits of our own behaviour, we make guilty of our disasters the sun, the moon, and stars; as if we were villains on necessity; fools by heavenly compulsion; knaves, thieves and (traitors) by spherical predominance; drunkards, liars and adulterers by an enforc'd

obedience or planetary influence; and all that we are evil in by a divine thrusting on.

He concludes by (a) recognising his own evil and (b) declaring that he would have been just as he is whatever celestial phenomena coincided with his conception. Right again, and no less so for the fact that he is (unlike Cassius) arguably the play's chief villain.

Superstition covers a multitude of sins – and that's *exactly* what they are for any ambitious student. Even if you despise astrological explanations as much as Edmund and I do, you may still believe it's a matter of sheer chance whether you'll get a fair examiner or a nasty one, whether the question will be to your taste or impossible to do, and – most of all – whether you'll have one of your good days or the reverse. All that is silly, self-wounding mumbo-jumbo – the kind of sub-thinking that jettisons all that makes you in charge. Becoming a high-flyer owes nothing to chance – apart from the admitted good fortune that you were born with a fine brain. Give thanks for that, if you like; the rest is a matter of applied reasoning, logic and organisation.

I've spent a fair time on superstition not just because it is an especially virulent danger for any student: as I hope is evident by now, it goes hand in hand with self-delusion of the saddest sort. And it helps fuel the further delusion that success hinges on 'showmanship'. That term may need explaining; it certainly deserves a section all to itself.

If superstition covers a multitude of sins, showmanship is hardly less broad in sweep. The term signifies any and all of:

1   an excessive regard for surface glitter;
2   the belief that stylish presentation is paramount;
3   the conviction that every last thing needs to be spelled out and/or showing off one's knowledge and reading;
4   a tendency to engage in arguments that look good initially but which are specious, spurious or just won't do;
5   a fondness for canny short-cuts.

And oddly enough:

6   A frequent reliance on structures and strategies which have not come naturally but have been taught – often unwisely.

As that last, somewhat singular item might indicate, show-manship is not usually the preserve of the conceited student who grandly wishes to share with everyone how clever s/he is. First, if my (fortunate) experience is any guide, there are few students of that kind anyway; those who really are that clever – and know it – tend also to be humble, more concerned with the work itself than with self-advertisement. Second, all the characteristics listed have their roots in ignorance accompanied by a nervous reverence for the 'mystique' of learning and exam-passing. Confident students will, by and large, just get on with it in a vigorous and forthright way; diffident students are quickly and easily persuaded that there exist magic elixirs to take all the pain and arduousness away if only they can find them.

Since points 4–6 are covered in some detail in Chapters 5 and 6, I shall not comment further on them now – though be on the look-out for them in your own work at all times: none of us is immune to the occasional flaw in those areas. What concerns me primarily at this early stage are points 1–3, simply because:

They imply that style matters more than content.

This is about the worst creed *any* student can embrace, let alone one looking to be a high-achiever.

On occasion during this book, I shall be making reference to Study Skills Lectures and Workshops that I have conducted away from my own schools and 'day job'. A major fringe benefit of running such sessions is that I often learn as much from the dele-gates as I am able to impart to them. That may not be all that financially just – they pay, I am paid – but I can assuage my guilt by passing on some of those lessons to you.

A recent commission was a five-hour Study Skills Day School held on a cold and damp March Saturday – and I don't need to tell you that any such attendees are *serious* aspirant high-flyers! I was impressed not only by their speed of response and their overall intelligence[9] but by what they were comfortable with and tuned into. And by what they were not. They were very strong on the following issues:[10]

1   The dangers of Study Aids. (Mind you, they were worryingly interested in websites as an elixir.)

2   Key Word Noting and noting techniques in general. They expressed prodigious boredom – and impatience – with 'Spidergrams', which is one reason why that (evidently) stale technique receives the barest coverage in Chapter 5!
3   Question decoding and not rushing into one's first, instinctive answer.

On the other hand, they:

4   Had received no instruction or advice about speed-reading.
5   Were/are deeply mistaken (in my view) about '*Introductions*'.
6   Point 3 above notwithstanding, seemed highly imprecise on 'command verbs' and their decisive significance in any examination.

I'll be revisiting all six issues subsequently. But these students exhibited one hang-up above all others:

'Presentation', whether in hand-written or word-processed form.

They came from a number of different institutions, yet almost to a man and woman they seemed to have had it drummed into them that how their work *looked* was of prime importance.

It was a tricky moment. We were all just there for the day, briefly intimate strangers; I was reluctant to counter directly what their teachers had said, partly out of professional caution but mainly because the last thing I wanted to do was erode their confidence and sense of security just eight weeks away from the most important exams in their lives so far. On the other hand, I knew they were *wrong*, and that unless they were disabused, the consequences for them could be very expensive. So in the end I felt impelled to point out that be it coursework, timed exams, dissertations, you name it:

There are no marks for 'Artistic Impression'.

There may be one or two obvious exceptions (Art itself, certain components of Design & Technology) but in the main academic tasks have nothing in common with Olympic Ice Dancing or Synchronised Swimming.

They were initially shocked (in one or two cases visibly annoyed) by this revelation. One young lady countered with the assertion that:

> **Poor presentation can *lose* you marks; if it's bad enough – illegible or so messy that the marker can hardly follow it – it could cause you to *fail*, let alone miss a top grade.**

She was quite correct, of course. But two things need to be said in return.

First, such extreme instances are very rare. Exam Boards and their markers are remarkably tolerant about legibility and mess: if it's readable, that's the end of the matter – and I mean 'readable', not 'lovely to look at'. Over the last five years I must have marked nearly 3,000 exam papers of one sort or another: only four qualified as truly illegible. As the young lady above surmised, all four failed. But then they should, shouldn't they? If you can't be bothered to take even minimal steps to communicate with your reader, you cannot complain if the latter refuses to go on pursuing the impossible.

Second, the fact that poor presentation can be penalised does not conversely mean that beautifully delivered work will get extra marks. It will certainly please the reader and thus create good will, but while that's not unimportant, it is not a 'scoring' issue. After all, even in Humanities subjects the allocation of marks to reward correct English is a pitifully small proportion of the overall tally;[11] given that, it's not surprising that matters of aesthetic appeal or 'impression' don't count at all.

Furthermore, the false prioritisation of presentation is not only uneconomic: it can lead to far worse problems and flaws. If you are *that* preoccupied with the visual aspects of a piece of work, I'm afraid the chances are that the content is going to suffer, often badly. Any teacher and marker you might ever meet will have plenty of mini-horror-stories about essays that look absolutely wonderful *until you begin reading them*. Eye-catching fonts, clever-but-unobtrusive graphics and illustrations, judicious use of highlighting features abound – accompanied by text that is awash with errors of all kinds and material that is at best pedestrian.

You cannot afford anything like this to tarnish your own work. That doesn't mean that you should stop caring about how your assignments look: good presentation is always better than bad! But turn your attention to such things *at the end*, not at the start. Keep intellectual control: get down on paper or the screen the main body of what you want to do. Then you can start polishing it – which includes editing it in properly lynx-eyed fashion. That means:

- Not mindlessly trusting the spellcheck but counter-checking it. You are in charge, and bossy software is often wrong or at any rate not necessarily right.
- Checking ruthlessly for typos: any that survive are *your* fault, not the PC's or your pen's.
- Checking your paragraphing. For a start, *is* there any? And if you have avoided that damaging absence, how long or frequent are those paragraphs? Do they assist the flow and bite of your work or hinder it?
- Then, and only then, with all basic and stylistic properties in good shape, you can 'tart up' the final submission via fancy fonts and so forth. I'm being neither facetious or condescending: such things genuinely enhance good work, I freely admit. But they are the icing on the cake, not its main ingredients.

All the above points apply just as much to hand-written work, with obvious technical difficulties. 'Handwriting' is a separate topic later on (see Chapter 5), so I won't dwell on it now. Suffice to say that beautiful copperplate orthography employed to communicate error-ridden drivel is just as bad as its font-and-graphics-obsessed PC equivalent.

Before leaving showmanship, I want to say a few words about the danger of feeling compelled to tell 'all you know'. Another 'outside' student once told me he'd been advised to think of examiners as essentially stupid or suspicious readers who require you to spell everything out in order to reward you fully. I was far from happy with that as a principle, though I did not say so then;[12] what mattered more immediately – on the evidence of several pieces of past work he later sent me for comment – was that it had led this young man into:

- prolixity as opposed to comprehensiveness;
- repetition rather than development – and thus, I fear ...
- ... tediousness instead of enlightenment.

It wasn't that he was in any way short on talent or under-informed; moreover, his commitment and sensitivity were most warming. But none of the specimens he sent me would have got a top grade in spite of his clear potential to achieve that. There was just too much of it all – long-winded introductions which said very little other than paraphrase the titles at inordinate length; yards of quotation that was either unanalysed or simply dupli-cated points already made in his text; and a general determination to leave no stone unturned or possible angle unconsidered that resulted merely in stagnation.

- Don't adopt such overkill methods.
- Be selective, and be sure that you keep aware of points you've already made.
- Above all, keep things as simple and punchy as possible: make every sentence say something you want it to.

Nobody admires or will give much credit to thin work, but that is most unlikely to be your problem at any time or in any subject. Your main goal should be to make your answers, whether in an exam or any other kind of assignment, as muscular and as clear as you can. Or, to offer another rather aggressive analogy, favour the rapier, not the bludgeon; be a sniper, not a blanket-bomber.[13]

I have not yet spent much time on smart-alec ruses. That is because, although they are just as damaging a 'drug' as the others, they tend to be indulged by weak, even inadequate students, not the kind I'm writing these pages for. Most such antics are as trans-parent as ineffective, and I would guess you've left them behind long ago, if indeed you ever descended to them. However, there is one smart-alec approach to which even the brightest students are prone, and such is its potential to wreak havoc that it qualifies as an 'S' word in its own right.

Spotting the question

Never give the slightest thought, credence or attention to any teacher who plays this shallow and pernicious game.

Okay, yes: it is possible to deduce that it is likely that question *x* may come up in some form or that topic *y* is likely to feature. That is as far as you can go; any attempt to go further is both futile and very dangerous.

You need to trust me here, and that's not necessarily an easy thing to do. You may have received contrary advice or comment; you are likely to have indulged in 'past paper detective work' with friends and peers, which is invariably a feature of pre-exam student behaviour; and you may have noticed stories about the whole matter in the press. Here's an example that is disturbingly instructive.

You may be aware that interest in and adoption of the International Baccalaureate is mushrooming. I understand that this is a global phenomenon, but its development in my own country has been startling. Five years ago the number of UK schools doing IB may have been in double figures, but only just; as I write (early 2005) there are over 100, with a similar number looking to adopt it in the next two years. There are probably several reasons for this, but undoubtedly one of them is widespread and increasing dissatisfaction with our domestic educational programmes.

As a result, it is not hard to imagine how embarrassed the Qualifications and Curriculum Authority[14] is by that surge of implemented interest in IB. And as so often happens, discomfiture has prompted attack. A piece appeared in *The Times* on Monday, 29 December 2003 headlined:

Pupils can guess the question in exam, says watchdog.

Its second paragraph read:

> **A report by QCA casts doubt on the claims that the IB is necessarily more rigorous and wide-ranging than the A level. It says that the structure offers more scope for students to question-spot, enabling them to follow a narrower course of study than is claimed.**

No evidence was offered to support these accusations, which is unsurprising, for none exists. The idea that the IB is 'narrower' than claimed – or by implication narrower than Curriculum 2000 – is simply not true. Moreover, QCA's spokesperson gave its real game away with this remarkable statement:

Because IB students cover six subjects – instead of an average of three for A-level students – the report also found that they had an average of an hour less of exams per subject.

So what? First, might not fewer exams in our testing-infested times be well worth celebrating on principle anyway? But second, and more important, are we really to assume that a course is 'broader' because it carries more exam-time at the end? Is that the depths to which the obsession with product has sunk?

I hope as high-flyers you find that account of interest and use. However, whether you do or not:

It raises matters of urgent relevance to you beyond such philosophical considerations.

Let us suppose I'm mistaken, and that QCA really do have a point about question-spotting. Again, so what? What QCA – and all incautious teachers and students who play that foolish game – do not seem to have grasped is that spotting the question is just the start: where do you go from there? Into deep trouble, that's where.

First, 'spotting the question' can only be general pursuit; it is in fact a perilously *vague* one. Yes, you might be correct in predicting a particular topic, feature or angle; however, every exam question is freshly and uniquely phrased. Specifically and crucially, the 'command verb' may be different from what you were anticipating. Here's a brief example to illustrate how precarious, even ruinous, such 'second guessing' can be:

Let's assume you're sitting a History exam, and that you've mugged up on 'the rise of Hitler' in the canny belief that the question will ask you to describe it. You open the paper, and great is your joy when half-way down the list of questions you read: *'Explain the rise of Hitler'*.

'It worked!' you silently yell to yourself in glee, and steam into your answer with the confident certainty of one whose number has come up.

That is essentially a true story, and I'm afraid the outcome was not what the student so blithely counted on. The question he was set differed – devastatingly – from the one he had banked on and proceeded to answer.

To *'describe'* the rise of Hitler means charting his progress within four years from an apparently insignificant maverick with delusions of grandeur to the elected leader of Germany. That will involve a study of how he effected this – how he manipulated the democratic process and managed to become the only democratically elected tyrant of the twentieth century. And so on. There is room here, naturally, for opinion, interpretation and selection of material, but at bottom you'll be dealing with facts, dates and numbers.

To *'explain'* the rise of Hitler requires you to *account for* that extraordinary phenomenon, not just *chart* it. That means (I would say) you have to look at the state of Germany when Hitler first appeared – a nation in desperate economic decline, at least partly caused by the draconian indemnity slapped on it by the victorious Allies in 1919. You would then perhaps dwell on the theory that extreme situations often provoke extreme measures and reactions, and that a nation in such dire straits would turn to anyone offering salvation, even a figure who in steadier times would be laughed to scorn.[15] That might in turn lead you into an investigation of the mass psychology of fascism, even into the suggestion that Hitler's rise proves as much about humankind as it does about 1930s Germany.

I am only an amateur historian at most, and I have no doubt that many of you who have just read my two 'answers' could furnish better ones. The real point, of course, is that *describe* and *explain* demand two quite different approaches and will draw on quite different material. There will be *some* overlap, naturally – but not enough to make the 'wrong' essay a true success. The student in question, hoping for an A*, got a B.

That story illustrates much more than the need to 'decode' the instructional verb you're given, vital though that task is (a comprehensive section on 'command verbs' can be found in Chapter 5 – see pp. 118–19). It also shows how the desire to out-smart the examiners can lead to complacency: once you've decided that this or that question will be there, the temptation is to think something along the lines of:

Sorted! Job done.

No it isn't. '*Spotting*' the question is not the same thing as '*doing*' it. Moreover, the great likelihood is that you will trot out a *prepared* answer, not quite as injuriously as our hapless History student, perhaps, but to your detriment nonetheless. One of the things an exam asks you to do – quite rightly, especially if you're a high-flyer – is show that you can think on your feet. Or to put it more augustly:

Show that you can adapt your knowledge to the precise criteria of any given task.

You're much less likely to do that to the full if you're focused on thinking you did days or weeks before.

Question-spotting confuses wise-guy tricks with learning and clarity of thought. High-flyers have the latter properties in abundance and they don't need the former poisoned chalice. And it *is* poisoned; quite apart from all the other venomous ingredients I've itemized, what happens if the question you and your advisers were sure would come up doesn't appear? Answer: immediate depression and/or panic – not exactly ideal states for someone looking for an optimum performance.

Now on to two more 'S' words: study aids and 'surfing the Net'.

The first need not detain us long. I've already made it amply clear what I think of the vast majority of these publications; all I need add is:

No would-be high-flyer needs them or indeed should touch them.

I'm not talking about decent text books and scholarly works: the former are essential and the latter highly desirable. My scorn is directed at those commercially produced 'Pass Notes' and the like that either duplicate what your texts, teachers and you are doing anyway or – worse and more often – subvert and contaminate by being badly-written, wrong-headed or just plain wrong. And even if you think that's coming on too strong, the fact remains that your success hinges on a:

A healthy partnership between your brain and your teachers'.

If you get that right, study aids are irrelevant. Save yourself a lot of time, boredom and money.

I suspect that 'surfing the Net' is a dated phrase now, and I apologise for my old-fogeyness. But the term remains useful for my purposes here, suggesting as it does a skimming, largely ludic (i.e. playful) activity. Now, there's nothing wrong with *play* as such: I'll be showing that on many occasions it can have an immensely productive role when studying. But you cannot afford to *confuse* work and play, to pretend you're doing real research when all you're doing is the website equivalent of TV channel-hopping. Because it's still relatively new and exciting, and also sexily fashionable, the Net can be dangerously seductive, conning you into three hours' browsing that is a waste of your time even if you download a lot of 'interesting looking' material.

It is dangerously seductive in two other ways as well. The first is its awesome size. It's not just that virtually every commercial, academic and political organisation on the planet has its own website; there are by now tens of millions of individuals who can say the same. And in truth its democratic nature is one of the Net's great virtues: anyone can publish on it. But it only takes a moment or two's thought, I trust, to see that this is also one of its vices, or at any rate a huge potential snare. Just because it's there doesn't mean it's reliable. Consequently:

You need to exercise great care and even greater judgement.

This is not difficult, in fact: after all, you are a Straight 'A's prospect. But I would advise you to make a conscious effort when consulting the Net to increase your level of concentration and scepticism: don't let the magic get to you! Ask yourself:

• Is this really any good?
• Can I check it out independently/confirm its reliability else-where?
• Is it truly relevant to what I'm doing? Does it add weight and authority to my own work?

If all the answers are affirmatives, great. But one last question remains, and it's the most important:

Is it *better* than anything I could do?

I am not encouraging arrogance in you, but remember, always, that you have a lot of talent and you shouldn't be shy about it. If the item you've unearthed really is strengthening, then by all means use it; however, I think you'll find that as often as not you'll do just as well on your own (see Appendix I for further observations and advice on the Internet and its use).

The phrase I've just written, 'by all means use it', also telegraphs the last of the Internet's dangers, and it can be a catastrophic one.

Plagiarism

Plagiarism is nothing more nor less than intellectual theft, and it can cost the student more dearly – certainly more dramatically – than any other of the vices and traps we've been investigating.

There are, I think, two kinds of plagiarism:

The cynical and the innocent.

The former culprits are either too lazy or too diffident (possibly both) to do any work themselves, simply ripping off whole swathes of others' efforts. That is not only or even mainly shabby: it is *very* stupid.

All writers have an individual voice, a perceptible stylistic signature. In the case of the beginner this may be halting and as yet raw, but it's still there, and anyone familiar with your work will recognise it. If you suddenly ape the style – and thinking – of an international authority, or even an Internet chancer whose stuff has mistakenly impressed you, it won't take a forensic scientist to spot what you've done. The great American writer Raymond Chandler had one of his characters observe, 'The wise guy never fools anybody but himself',[16] and nowhere is that more the case than in acts of cynical plagiarism.

'Innocent' plagiarism may be less morally disreputable but it's just as damaging. This comes about through a different kind of laziness born of bad organisation and resulting in last-minute panic: yes, you meant to acknowledge this source and that quotation, but you were past your assignment deadline and you didn't have time. There is only one answer to that – well, only one they'll let me print – and it is:

Rubbish.

Footnotes, acknowledgements and a bibliography are as much a part of your assignment as its title and the main text itself. In addition, even if your marker believes your feeble sob-story, you're still going to be down-graded for the fault.

My last point about plagiarism is introduced by the words of a friend and highly experienced colleague:

> **'By now it is much easier for pupils to nick things than it is for us to determine where or from whom it was nicked.'**

Partly because they have grown up with the Net rather than adapted to it in middle age (never easy!), teenage students are much more proficient at 'lifting' material than are teachers, markers and examiners at establishing its provenance. There *are* some effective police forces around – notably the website www.turnitin.com., used by many IB schools, all universities in the UK and a vast number of American colleges and universities worldwide. But in truth, the cops are never going to catch up with the robbers here; for a start, they're outnumbered.

That is not offering you a licence to steal! Quite the reverse: what I've just been discussing is the most dangerous snare of all. It may be true that the cops will never catch *all* the robbers, but they will catch *some*. You don't want to be in that number, do you? Being caught out, whatever you've done, is always humiliating, but that's not the worst thing that might happen if you plagiarise. You could have your work disqualified – and not just in the perpetrated subject but right across the board. This really is a case where honesty is the best policy. It's also the simplest one, allowing you to get on with showing how good you are, guilt-free and fully focused.

Before closing, one last 'S' word:

Spellcheck

I've briefly mentioned this highly double-edged facility already. In her admirable *From Notepad to Mousepad* Judith Woolf advises students to

> **learn to use a spell-check. *Learn* is the operative word here.**

The italics are mine, not the author's: evidently, I consider the point even more important than she does![17] If you don't do as she says, spellcheck will become another destructive drug, not an aid. Your brain must stay **in charge**, for I'm afraid that:

Computers don't do context.

Conclusion

A good deal of this chapter may have struck you as negative, bossy, severe or all three. I can't say that has been my intention, but I'm not too displeased if that *is* your response – provided that you're still looking to read on!

One of the greatest pleasures of teaching really bright students – or writing for them, as I am here – is that there is no need to be *kind*. Not that I dislike being kind, you understand: kindness is indeed one of the greatest of human qualities, blessing both giver and receiver. But it is nevertheless liberating to cater for those who are strong enough to be told things without adornment, whose confidence is not fragile, and who know that the more they are forewarned, the better they will perform. I have paid you the compliment of including you in that select group – people who actually appreciate tough talking as an asset rather than a rebuke.

Most of the rest of what now follows is much more cheerful, positive and, I hope, both entertaining and enabling. I've started in this largely stern way in the profound belief that the aspirant high-flyer can be swayed by seemingly attractive strategies that are actually either irrelevant detours or actively damaging. I hope you now have a sound grasp of where you stand and how things currently are in the world you inhabit. As I observed earlier, students are pressured as never before, and perhaps that is especially so if you have high aims and large goals. However, if you steer clear of the perils to which this chapter has been mainly devoted, that pressure should ease, leaving you freer to go for it in a more relaxed and secure fashion. Now let's see how you can further arm yourself – and have a good deal of fun in the process.

Chapter 2

Using it

Arming yourself

By now it should be clear that I am assuming that anyone who has picked up (or preferably bought!) a book entitled *Getting Straight 'A's* is more than likely to be:

Clever
Ambitious
Hungry to learn as well as to succeed.

That amalgam also signals, I would imagine, a lot of confidence, which is very good. But to fulfil the target enshrined in my title you will need to take full note of another three-pronged formula:

Honesty → Vanity → Caring

They may not interlock in quite the same was as do enjoyment, confidence and success, but they are all essential weapons for any ambitious student. Let's consider them one by one.

Honesty

Utterly necessary, and in several ways.

First, it means 'owning up' when you do not know or understand something. This is never easy for a student to do, especially in a class where, one feels, admission of ignorance will invite peer-ridicule. The fact that those peers hardly ever *do* ridicule you is not the point:

It is *the fear that they might* which makes you keep quiet.

Having experienced that fear many times, I am entirely sympathetic to it. On the other hand, it won't do. A teacher can only help you fully if s/he is aware of what you don't understand or know, and why. If you keep a proud silence, you harm rather than arm yourself, not least because you're failing to *use* your teacher properly.

Second, it means being switched on to your states of mind and body. It is, for example, foolish to work when you're dog-tired:

- For obvious reasons, you won't do that work very well.
- That will sap your confidence; in addition you'll probably have to re-do the work at another time – which is irritating, humiliating, or both.
- The short- and medium-term effects on your enjoyment and confidence will be entirely negative.

So if you are not in shape to work, be thankfully honest about it and either go to bed or chill out.

On the other hand, such state-of-the-student honesty has a tougher application as well. You must not *pretend*. If you're feeling sluggish or just lazy rather than truly tired, you need to kick yourself out of it and use the energy which (underneath you know perfectly well) is ready and waiting. All of us are staggeringly inventive at making excuses; the straight 'A's student cannot afford to indulge them very often, if at all.

Honesty also involves being true to yourself – to your opinions, your responses and your instincts. You should of course avoid complacency here, let alone smugness (although see pp. 26–9 on vanity); however, in my experience that is hardly ever the problem. What causes trouble, especially early on in a course, is that students are not *certain* about how they feel or what they think, causing them to doubt the validity of their response and to hide behind the views of others – teachers, authors, even their classmates. Again, that is understandable, but it is neither sensible nor necessary, for it is overwhelmingly likely that you will change your mind about this or that during your course, and you may do so many times. But you can't productively change your mind unless you know what you're changing it *from*. So stay alert at all times to your own views and 'take' on things.

A major benefit of such alert clarity is that you will avoid the trap of wondering, 'What do they want me to say?'. Especially dangerous in an examination, this is wrong thinking from the outset – and my objection is practical, not moral. The real point about pursuing a 'line' that you hope will please the reader/examiner is not that it's dishonest but that *it doesn't work*. If your heart isn't in it, neither will your brain be – or not enough of it, anyway.

There is one more aspect to honesty which may seem markedly philosophical but is in fact a sound practical truth:

All good students are *humble*, but few of them are *modest*.

A good mind knows what it does not know and where it is not strong. As the amount of information and knowledge increases – and it's now doing so faster than ever before – such good minds are going to be even more aware of their vast deserts of ignorance. That may be hard to contemplate, but it's also the first determined step to transforming as much as possible of those deserts into cultivated knowledge.

The clear-sighted and simultaneous recognition of what one doesn't know and what one does is a good working definition of 'humility'. Its alleged counterpart, 'modesty', can actually become its enemy, or at any rate the enemy of the hungry student. Nobody likes a swank, but the reluctance to recognise your own quality can be highly injurious to you. It's an insidious process: you may begin by understating your achievements in a charming manner, but unless you're careful and remain fully switched on to those achievements, you can start to believe your own publicity, losing a lot of impetus and determination as a result. It is no accident that we also use the word 'modest' to describe something unremarkable or, frankly, not much good. That is not an outcome that anyone reading this book will find attractive, and avoiding it is primarily a matter of *attitude*.

The distinction I've been making is important anyway, and it also ushers in the second essential item in the high-flyer's psychic armoury.

Vanity

While honesty has always been regarded as one of the prime virtues, I have never seen vanity referred to as anything other than a vice. That is part of a centuries-old puritanism which is still remarkably virulent; I hope it will prove divertingly valuable to offer an alternative and in some respects subversive view.

From devout Christian to resolute atheist and every shade of belief in between, most of Western mankind is alerted – usually at a tender age – to the 'Seven Deadly Sins'. Just for the record, they alphabetically comprise:

Anger   Avarice   Envy   Gluttony   Lust   Sloth   Vanity

The interesting thing about this septet is that, with one exception,[1] they are all – *up to a point* – pleasurable and enabling. The two kinds of greed, 'avarice' (material possessions, wealth) and 'gluttony' (food and drink) may have inspired moralists and satirists to paint, in pictures or words, hideous and disgusting portraits of these vices' most excessive manifestations. Yet wouldn't we all rather live in a well-appointed and comfortable house, have enough money, eat and drink both well and wisely, rather than camp out on the streets in constant penury and danger of starvation? Nice things are always nicer than nasty ones, and in most instances a lot better for you too.

Everyone knows how destructive 'anger' can be, and not just when it boils over into murderousness or something approaching it. To be enclosed in a room with someone in a rage is always highly uncomfortable at best, even if you're not the actual target. Yet anger can also be liberating and apposite. Shakespeare's Lear speaks of 'noble anger' and the phrase is an illuminating one. There are times when it is *right* to be angry – when one sees injustice, or wanton cruelty, or a whole host of similarly despicable things. Unvaried placidity and moderation-in-all-things temperance are less admirable than is sometimes supposed; besides, for most of us they are impossible anyway.

A similar caution needs to be exercised over 'sloth'. To be sure, the couch-potato-slob who needs half an hour's rest after blowing his nose is among humankind's less admirable specimens, and the mixture of physical inertia plus mental torpor that is sloth is a very bad lifestyle option, not least because it must surely be terminally dull. But in an age characterised by a near-manic belief in 'hard work', the occasional slump into cretinous inactivity not only has attractions but unbridled virtues. Anyone who has a busy, pressed life knows how luxurious – and very good for you – can be a day or so of pure sloth. And while in the interests of decorum I'll restrict my observations on 'lust' to a bare (ha ha) minimum, I will say that anyone who thinks such an impulse invariably wicked and to be shunned has, or is going to have, a rather forlorn life in more ways than one.

The point I've been moving towards in the foregoing paragraphs is that:

> **Six of those 'deadly sins' are nothing of the kind unless they get out of control. Or to put it more precisely, until things reach a stage where they control *you*.**

Only then do they become fatal, not least because in such an extreme form each one is invariably compounded by the 'Eighth Deadly Sin', *'stupidity'*.

Before I finally get to vanity, let's consider its close cousin pride. We're all taught very early on that 'pride comes before a fall', and vainglorious self-puffing is indeed highly precarious; it is additionally unwise in rendering the culprit both ridiculous and friendless. Hang on a minute, though. What about such remarks as 'I'm very proud of you'; 'He takes an admirable pride in his work'; 'You should be very proud of that performance'? Don't those suggest that pride can be unambiguously laudable, either as an inner strength or an apposite accompaniment to deserved achievement?

Though I say it myself, vanity fits into this enquiry in the neatest possible way. Just like its five companions, it unquestionably becomes a vice once out of control, whether the vanity in question is looking-glass narcissism or less visible forms of self-preening. Beyond that critical point, it resembles pride in making the victim both ludicrous and thoroughly disagreeable, as are all people who inhabit a universe of one. Moreover, vanity of such proportions is of course always deluded:

> **Not for nothing does the term 'in vain' denote *failure*.**

Yet all students need and will be nourished by their proper share of vanity – controlled, yes, but undoubtedly *there*. One reason is that its presence will make you determined not to make a mess of anything you do. Yes, you'll do so occasionally, like all of us. But arguably the biggest difference between those who are truly committed about what they do and those who finally just play at it is:

The former absolutely *hate* screwing up.

It offends their professional self-esteem and you can bet it fuels their determination not to get caught out again. That, it seems to me, is another unambiguously good quality – and vanity is the source and provider.

Next, a more positive side-effect, and a very warming one. Down the years I have been struck by how many people who are 'vain' in the healthily controlled way I'm advocating tend also to be generous in their response to and view of others. That should surprise only those who insist on considering 'vices' and 'virtues' as moral concepts only, rather than as psychological states as well. For if you feel good about yourself – or 'vain', if you wish – you are much more likely to recognise quality and worth in others, if only because such strengths do not threaten you.[2] And that kind of open-heartedness is of enormous value to an ambitious student. As I'll be observing in Chapter 3, over the duration of a course students learn as much from each other as they do from their teachers. You are much more likely to gain such benefits if you're genuinely and generously interested in what others have to say.

The final virtue of vanity is that it gives you added steel if and when things are not going as well as you want them to, or people are suggesting to you that they're not. I observed earlier that part of the pleasure of success lies in confounding those who doubted or dismissed you, and vanity has its part to play in bringing that about. Indeed, for all that I stand by my pronouncement that enjoyment is the student's most priceless asset, it is remarkable what a judicious mixture of anger and vanity can effect! I can tell you that it helped me get my Ph.D, and it will help many of you to get all those 'A's.

Now on to the last of the high-flyer's trinity.

Caring

The word 'care' has several meanings or applications. One of them – 'looking after the afflicted or disadvantaged' – is not relevant to the ambitious student; all the rest are central.

First, there is *care* as in 'burden', the sense of being ground down by worry or responsibility. The Victorian poet W.H. Davies put it perfectly:

> *What is this life, if full of care,*
> *We have no time to stand and stare?*

That usage of the noun is now rare; however, its meaning survives in the still-current adjectives '*careworn*' and '*carefree*'. They are of course opposites. The first means ground down by worry, responsibility and anxiety – a state every student will want to avoid. The second means the absence of all those debilitating concerns – a state every student will want to cultivate. So make the latter your aim. That is not to suggest that everything will go like a breeze or that you won't at times feel somewhat weighed down; however, if you take good note of the advice in this book (especially concerning matters of organization) those moments will be infrequent.

Next, the verb '*to take care of*' as in 'accomplish'. The most apposite phrase for our purposes is 'taking care of business' – seeing to the unglamorous but essential tasks which are a large part of any activity. During a student's life there are obvious peaks and prime targets – major coursework assignments, assessed practicals and/or oral presentations, and of course exams. But these actually account for a surprisingly small amount of your study-time and work-requirements:

Most of what you do will be private, non-assessed, exploratory.

Or put in a nutshell, *learning* as opposed to *performing*. If you take care of all such quieter matters in an efficient, no-nonsense way, those eventual peaks and targets will be readily accessible.

Most important of all, though, is 'care' as a verb, meaning 'to bother, to mind' and also 'to feel fondness for'. It hardly needs saying that any student who does not or cannot feel those things is in serious trouble from the outset, but I've made a point of saying it because:

Not only is such an attitude vital: nobody else can do it for you.

Teachers, parents, friends and myriad non-human resources can all help you a great deal, but they are powerless unless the impulse to give serious and affectionate attention to your work is deep-rooted within you. Vanity will assist you here, as will honesty, especially on those forgivable occasions when you *don't* care very much and need to take a break from the whole thing. In the end, though, you will be best sustained by the fact that it really matters to you to do things as well as you can. The great French thinker Voltaire once suggested that 'the best is the enemy of the good', which you could do worse than adopt as a form of motto:

Committed high-flyers are not satisfied with getting by or even doing pretty well; they're not even interested in 95 per cent.

Adding the final 5 per cent invariably hinges on:

How much you truly want it.

My final observations in this section put the spotlight on '*careless*'. The adjective is used so often – all students (including this one) have had it hurled at them at one time or another – that its currency has been devalued or, rather, its true significance is rarely grasped.

As I've already observed, we all make mistakes, and on occasion those mistakes are seriously embarrassing. The latter are, naturally, always regrettable, and avoiding them is one of the benefits of conscientious 'checking and editing', which I address in Chapter 5. Yet even those do not constitute *fully fledged* carelessness, which signifies a prevailing attitude rather than a sudden blip:

True carelessness is *chronic*.

It's not just the odd slip but several per paragraph. It's not just a lazy dependence on spell-check facilities but a disinclination to ensure that your sentences make full and clear sense. It's not just the omission of a few desirable punctuation points but an indifference to whether the reader can comfortably follow what you're looking to say. And sometimes it's not just the inclusion of rather tenuous arguments, points or quotations but the failure to deal with what the question asks or what the task requires.

All such flaws indicate someone who, ultimately and disastrously, simply does not care enough in that above sense of
'bother' or 'mind'. Students tend to resent that accusation when
levelled at them, arguing that in the majority of cases their errors
are minor, superficial ones that may slightly stain the overall
product but do not significantly damage it. The more I teach,
review and examine, the less disposed I am to go along with that
defence. The evidence is near-overwhelming: writers indifferent to
the little things invariably prove indifferent – i.e. mediocre – in
all the major ways too. In sum, for the ambitious high-flyer:

Carelessness = Doom

Knowing yourself

By happy chance, the acronym 'HVC' which denotes Honesty,
Vanity and Caring also signals a fourth property crucial to top-
flight success:

High-voltage Consistency

Ideally, you should work with a kind of quiet, controlled intensity. Over a lengthy course, however, that is not always possible;
even so, you should aim at very clear focus every time, be it a
class or a period of private study. That will be much easier to
achieve if your work-patterns are regular and their rhythm natural
and comfortable. And to help you effect *that*, it will greatly assist
you if the answers to these questions are firmly fixed in your mind:

1   Do you work best in the morning; the afternoon; the evening?
2   What is your normal concentration span when working on
    something you really enjoy and/or comes easily to you?
3   What is your normal concentration span when working on
    something that is less congenial or which you find problematic?
4   How often do you look over your past work, and for how
    long?
5   How would you rate your memory?
6   How good are your note-taking skills?
7   How often do you emend or update your notes?
8   Are you usually on time in submitting assignments?
9   Do you have enough time for rest and recreation?

In most cases, there are no 'right answers' as such; or to put it another way the 'right answer' is the one you have given – *provided you act on it*. There is advice on how best to effect that in Chapter 3.

If you are not yet sure of your answer in some instances, do not be concerned. This book's ultimate purpose is that you will finish it with all those and many other questions clearly answered and firmly established in your mind, equipping you for across-the-board success, and all the matters raised above are explored in detail later on. My reason for raising them at this preliminary stage is that, like that double HVC requirement, they allow you to arm yourself for all the challenges ahead. For everything I've discussed so far is pithily summarised in the two injunctions imposed by the founding father of philosophy, Socrates:

1   Know yourself.
2   Be yourself.

It intrigues me that the first is much better known, or at any rate much more often quoted, than the second. Perhaps this is because 'know yourself' implies humility, whereas 'be yourself' could appear to recommend 'selfishness'.[3] But Socrates was absolutely right to give equal weight to each; moreover, he knew that the two properties are symbiotic – that is, they interlock and are mutually nourishing. There's not much point in acquiring full self-knowledge if you don't *do* anything with it, allowing it to shape your actions, choices and life; otherwise you end up as a navel-gazer of no use to anyone, especially yourself. Conversely, to 'be yourself' without any understanding of what that self *is* quickly degenerates into oafish instinctualism, devoid not only of sensitivity to others but any idea of why you're doing what you're doing when you're doing it.

The great truths of life have not changed much since *Homo sapiens* crawled out of the primeval slime, and that dual Socratic command would be a prime proof. It is as fundamentally enabling to the twenty-first century student as it was to an Ancient Greek audience.[4] I won't say there's *nothing* you can't achieve once you've followed both guidelines to the full, but you're unlikely to be dissatisfied with what does come your way as a result. In addition, you will enter adulthood far more mature than many people twice your age. 'Growing up' means, ultimately, coming fully to terms with your own nature and acting on it. Not bad if you can do that before your teens are over: some people *never* make it however long they live.

Advancing yourself

In the Preface, I somewhat forbiddingly listed seven things this book will not or cannot do for you. Here's your side of it – a complementary summary of what you *can* do for yourself, five keys to getting it right and unlocking those straight 'A's.

1   Organisation is paramount

Nobody wants to turn you into a robot (least of all me) but you will save an immense amount of time, potential hassle and above all energy if you manage your time effectively in keeping with your biological and work rhythms.

You need also to ensure that the materials you need are immediately to hand. That means your work-files and resources just as much as mundane things like paper, pens and a properly serviced PC.

2   Look to learn from everyone and everything

There is nobody on earth who can't give you some form of valuable instruction, and all that you do – however tenuous its relationship to your life as a student may seem – can make you more informed and thus more assured.

3   Get 'hard work' into its proper perspective

It is a truism that nobody achieves anything worthwhile without a lot of effort. On the other hand, the converse notion that anything is achievable through industry alone is *not* true: it is, in fact, nonsense. The most one can say is this – a wise remark once pinned to the players' dressing room at Derbyshire County Cricket Club by the team's physiotherapist:

Hard work will always beat talent if talent doesn't work.

Indeed so. But the implicit point there is that talent is the source of everything, and the idea that hard work will on its own create and supply high-level aptitude is among the more fatuous myths of current Western society.

4 Concentrate instead on working well

Ambitious students can at times work *too* hard. That includes the mistake I discuss above under Honesty, but it can also involve worrying feverishly at a problem when the best thing to do is leave it alone and return to it later, or the strenuous belief when finishing off an assignment that just one more paragraph or just two more references will absolutely clinch things for you. Quality and clarity are all important; pedestrian time-serving or saturation-diligence are not what successful study is about.

5 Always look for connections and links

I'm sure you regularly do this in your individual subjects. To a certain extent that is built into all decent syllabuses anyway, and your teachers doubtless encourage it in order to give your learning breadth as well as depth.

Don't stop there, however. As well as looking to increase your reading and knowledge wherever you can, try to look at your entire programme of study as '*laterally*' as possible: you'll be surprised and even excited to find how often discrete subjects are mutually illuminating.

So don't think along the lines of 'Oh, that's English; nothing to do with Geography, Physics or Maths'; you'll probably be wrong, as these three connections exemplify:

- Physics and Literature are a lot closer than most people imagine: in their different ways, both explore the fundamental laws of life.
- Geography can often illuminate History, and vice versa.
- It is remarkable how often basic arithmetic can cast important light on a literary text – how many lines a given character has, how long a writer's paragraphs are and why, how many speaking parts this play has compared to that one and why that might be significant; and so forth.

To put it another way and to extend the point:

Guard against literal-mindedness when it comes to 'relevance'.

It would be overstating the case to suggest that *everything* is relevant to a hungry-to-learn and engaged student, but not by much. For one of the things that distinguishes the really classy mind is the ability to discern relevance and connections in the unlikeliest things, and to get others to see that too.

All these matters are explored further in later chapters.

I bring 'Using it' to a close by identifying one more key weapon in your armoury. Like virtually everyone, including those who would be embarrassed or aghast to admit it:

You have a dirty mind.

That may not be something you'll want to boast about, but it is, believe me, a major plus. It will help you to make connections and to remember things that otherwise resist your memory. It will allow you to learn from the most unlikely sources and situations and naturally recharge that high-voltage energy so central to top-flight achievement. Subsequent material explores precise ways in which you can bring this raunchiness to work for you; in the meantime and from now on, start 'using it', or at any rate get used to the fact of it. Quite apart from anything else, it will provide you with a lot of fun – and for any student, that is a priceless asset in itself.

Now on to 'Sorting it', focusing on self-management, organisation, concentration and other essential tools of the student's trade.

Chapter 3

Sorting it

> In my opinion we don't devote enough scientific research to finding a cure for jerks.
>
> Bill Larson

This first of three sections centres on '*self-management*'. Most of it is straightfoward, even obvious, but it would not be wise to skip it in the belief that you're above such things. No doubt that is true in many respects, and areas, but I also know how many people – including me – make a horlicks of something because they have ignored the obvious and been thoroughly unsensible.

Self-management I: get to know your brain

I do mean *your* brain. This is neither the time nor the place to dwell in detail on the marvellous, often still-mysterious properties of the kilogram of fine tissue that resides between our ears, fascinating though such neurological exploration can be. All I want to do is identify three things about your 'grey matter' which will increase your in charge control.

First and foremost:

Your brain is wonderful – and *immeasurably* better than any computer yet devised/manufactured or improbably imagined.

There will be further chapter and verse on that as we go along; for now, just *believe* it.

Second:

Your brain and body work together; understand your bio-rhythms.

Don't be put off by that last term. It simply denotes the way your body behaves across a day, a week or whatever, and if you've absorbed and answered the questions posed in the previous chapter about when you work best and so forth, you will already be suitably familiar with them. All you now need to do is *act on those answers,* making them the basis of your personal timetable and all aspects of 'scheduling'.

Naturally, a good deal of your activity is determined *for* you by the institution you attend – classes, lectures, seminars, so forth. At those times your bio-rhythms will have to cope as best they can – and as you doubtless know, they will do so pretty well. But a large and arguably the most crucial part of your study is *private,* and it is then that self-regulation comes to the fore.

I briefly mentioned 'concentration spans' in Chapter 2. This has become something of a 'buzz term' in education-speak, which is both good and bad. It is good in that almost everyone is much more aware than (say) twenty years ago of the need to:

- take breaks in classes;
- take breaks during private study;
- tailor tasks to one's natural work-rhythms.

It is bad in that it has persuaded many students and teachers that understanding one's patterns of attentiveness and alertness is all there is to it, guaranteeing a high level of efficient concentration and, thereby, successful learning. Once again, that is not so. The overall phenomenon of concentration is far from obvious or simple, and it troubles me that what began as *guidelines* have in certain circles come to acquire the status of *rules,* even *commandments.* Unsurprisingly, concentration spans are as individual, and therefore as variable, as bio-rhythms themselves. It is generally true, yes, that:

Most people work best at most things for somewhere between 20 and 35 minutes.[1]

But it is equally true that:

For most people most of the time and in most activities, that span will rarely be a *constant*.

There is no need to be confused or bothered by those two apparently opposing truths. Far from it: they should enable a healthy flexibility based on identifying:

* for how long you work well at a subject or topic you like;
* for how long you work well at a subject or topic that you don't like or find difficult;
* whether your concentration span differs according to the time of day or the day of the week.

And when you've done that:

* Build all of it into your schedule and work-management.

Another contemporary 'buzz term':

Go with the flow

sums it up very neatly. You will know when you're working really well and also when everything is sluggish and elusive. In the former case, just stay with it; in the latter, give yourself a break or do something else, and return to the task in question at another time when you're fresher and more positive.

My third and last tip in 'get to know your brain' is:

Think of your brain as an engine or as a muscle.

Engines and muscles are at their best when working, and they become more efficient as a result. They have other, subtler properties that are also highly analogous to the way your brain works and how you can use it to maximum advantage.

Just as an engine or one's muscles take a while to 'warm up', so does the brain, even if it reaches full effectiveness much faster. More importantly, when engines and muscles *stop* doing their work, they also take a while to 'turn off' completely. That is equally true of the brain – which offers a major potential benefit to every student in terms of 'Review and Revision'. Those vital concerns are mainly addressed in this book's final chapter, but you can do yourself an enormous favour by using that 'brain wind-down' period at the end of a work-session to:

Look over all – or at least a *selection* – of your past work.[2]

That may sound a forbidding and lengthy task: it isn't. You need spend only ten minutes on it, at which time your brain will be completely relaxed and you can turn to other things. But those ten minutes will:

1   quickly refresh your memory of what you have studied and 'logged';
2   very possibly prompt a new thought or insight;
3   boost your confidence by revealing (a) how much you've done; (b) how much you know; (c) how far you've already come.

Best of all, such regular review will mean that when you come to final pre-exam revision, you'll be in charge of a large proportion of what you need to know and deploy; that 'final lap' will be a matter of polishing and/or filling in a few remaining gaps. As a result your revision period will be as far from a nightmare as could reasonably be imagined; it may even prove a *pleasure*.[3]

Self-management II: equipment and assets

Equipment

It is a matter of much – and in my view useless[4] – debate whether the current generation of students is *more* knowledgeable, intelligent, committed, diligent, streetwise and whatever and so forth than its predecessor or *less* so. But of one thing there can be no doubt:

You lot have a hell of a lot more 'kit' than our lot did!

When I was a schoolboy, things had moved on a bit from the days when slate + some kind of writing implement was the sum total of a pupil's equipment, but when I look at the stuff my own students cart around on a daily basis,[5] that terminally overworked phrase 'light-years difference' springs to mind. Vast warehouse-outlets on every business park in the land pander to students' every possible need, supplying:

- pens of every conceivable variety and colour;
- plastic wallets of at least fifteen different types and operational design;
- highlighters;
- India rubber erasers – plus Tippex bottles, Tippex pens, Tippex mice;
- hole-punchers, staplers, forty-six different kinds of paper clip;
- box files, cardboard wallets, presentation folders.

Plus, in either that same shop or the PC emporium next door:

- computers; laptops; palm-tops; electronic note-pads;
- not to mention mobile phones, texting facilities, audio-visual messaging or any other such.

I'm not at all the grumpy old man such listings might suggest. On the contrary, I think they're great: not only useful and fun, they really can help make your work better organised and more attractive. But two warnings:

- Don't let them be an activity-unto-itself backwater.
- Stay in charge of them always. Make sure you know where they are, whether they're ready to work or need repairing/replacing. Like all aids, 'kit' is a good servant but a tyrannical master.

That last remark is especially true of computers and all similarly sophisticated gadgets, and these need a brief section to themselves.

Techno pitfalls

I've already issued a couple of warnings about PC-dependency – the specific dangers of spellcheck and the more general observation that computers cannot think – and there's another one coming up soon about the ruinously bad habits email can get you into if

you're not careful. It is therefore high time that I recorded my
enthusiasm for the PC and what it has engendered. Computers:

* are fun;
* are sexy;
* have enabled all of us to do a great number of important
  chores immeasurably faster than used to be the case;
* have raised standards of presentation, professionalism and
  user-friendly attractiveness;
* have given every owner a built-in, massive and instantly available memory-bank.

All that is to be celebrated, especially if you're a student.

However, like anything attractive and powerful, the PC can also
be dangerous. First of all:

PCs *have* been known to crash!

This is at best irritating; at worst it can be near-catastrophic. So:

**Back-up all your hard-drive material on disc, and
update regularly.**

Yes, I know everyone tells you to do this; I am also aware that
it is a great bore, especially if (as is usually the case) you've got
much more interesting stuff to do. But to lose vital material is a
great deal worse than boring, so grit your teeth and do it.

Second – and here I speak as both delegate and presenter –
'techno-screw-up' is such a frequent phenomenon as to qualify as
a law:

**Whether engaged on private study or a public
presentation, each additional piece of techno-
equipment that you depend on multiplies the
likelihood that one or other such gizmo will fail.**

It does not matter whether you attribute that law to Palmer or
to Sod: the point is to avoid such an eventuality at virtually all
costs. Not normally a punter, I would nevertheless bet a hefty
sum that anyone who decides to utilise

PowerPoint + DVD + Audio Cassette + Slide Projector

is asking for big trouble and will almost certainly get it.

That is not to sneer at those (valuable) facilities but to suggest you be wary of them anyway, and also make sure you have fail-safe back-up in the form of the printed word or, best of all, your own expertise and the consequent ability to just *talk*, fluently and with authority. One of the best television programmes I ever saw featured the great historian A.J.P. Taylor exploring the origins of the First World War. He was stationed in front of a blackboard – which was his only 'visual aid' (used very sparingly at that). No interactive whiteboards, no PowerPoint, not a bell or whistle in sight: just an oldish guy talking about something he knew about and wanted us to know about. And:

He was utterly riveting.

While none of us can claim his level of intellect, that performance embodied three lessons that every student should take note of:

*   There is never any substitute for real knowledge and expertise.
*   There is far less need than seems currently fashionable for 'bells and whistles' effects and graphic enhancement.
*   Ultimately, content *always* matters more than style.

A further, quick word about PowerPoint. That facility, so sexily state-of-the-art just a few years ago, now strikes many people as not only tedious but, worse, *lazy*. It has become the electronic equivalent of the flip-chart or the spidergram. Like any facility, it is worth considering; but it must *be* considered, not employed on a knee-jerk basis. And if you do use it:

Don't fall into the trap which ensnares many presenters – additionally issuing the audience with hard copy of everything and taking you through all of it in a cat-sat-on-the-mat fashion.

Audiences will put up with being bored; they hate being patron-ised. Granted, it is wise to have hard-copy back-up in case of electronic failure. But that is not at all the same thing as stuffing a multiple package down the audience's throat as Plan A. Such a policy, not only extremely dull but ruinously condescending, is witless abuse of a device that ought to excite and enable. In short, it is a recipe for audience-turn-off on a grand scale – hence the increasingly heard phrase 'Death By PowerPoint'.

Enjoy your computer – it is right, proper and hugely advantageous that you do so. But stay in charge of it: more than any other aspect of student life and aspirant success, the PC needs to know who is boss.

Three further assets

I don't want to be lazy any more than I want you to be, but I'll assume you're suitably primed about the colossal resources available to you via libraries, the Internet and indeed good old-fashioned books.[6] My purpose here is to encourage you to make full use of:

- your teachers;
- your fellow-students;
- your instincts.

Teachers

Teachers are one of your biggest resources – so exploit them. They are *paid* to be bothered, to be asked questions, to help you. Of course, there will be times when they are tired or very busy or really not all that interested in talking to you at length: you need to choose your moment with some care. On the other hand, any teacher who *consistently* fobs you off is failing in his/her job, and you should make that known to your institution. That takes a good deal of courage, but in the unlikely event that it's necessary, you really must do it – for others' sake as well as your own.

Those last two sentences strike an unwarrantedly negative note, as my use of 'unlikely' implies. The great majority of teachers are delighted to be asked intelligent questions and solicited for advice: it's why we went into this business in the first place. Moreover, the one thing that utterly frustrates teachers is when their students *don't* ask when they're puzzled, *don't* admit to not understanding something. We can codify that as something approaching an axiom:

Teachers cannot serve you fully unless and until they are aware of what you don't know. They are not mind-readers: *you* have to supply that information.

It isn't easy to 'own up' to ignorance in class. Your peer group[7] will I hope contain many friends, but it will also contain rivals, even the occasional enemy – and to lay yourself bare to those possibly hostile reactions takes some doing. But it must be done if you want to progress fully.

The same goes for oral contributions in class, be they asked-for responses or questions that you raise yourself. Some students find this easier and more natural than others. If you are shy or diffident, breaking that 'sound barrier' can be quite an ordeal – which any decent teacher recognises and respects:

1   I have never thought I could turn introverts into extroverts by *insisting* that they contribute vocally.
2   I would never subject shy students to such needless and cruel pressure anyway. It's *their* lesson as much as (if not more than) mine, and provided they're taking things in, how they do it is nobody else's business but theirs.

However, I would still say that the best way for good students to get even better is to 'test' themselves in public by hazarding ideas in class, by seeing and hearing the impact of their immediate (and as yet not fully formed) responses. Those ideas and responses will be – believe me – a long way distant from rubbish, and you will gain respect for both your bravery and your insight. Even more valuable, though, will be the *private* benefit you gain. The novelist E.M. Forster remarked:

How do I know what I think till I see/hear what I say?

That approximates a mantra for any high-flying student. *Use* your classes – which includes your teacher's conduct of them – to grow, to find out what it is you want to say when it comes to all those crunches, be they coursework, exams or vivas.

Fellow-students

Making full use of each other is as important as making full use of your teachers. That may seem a superfluous observation: after all, students spend a great deal of time talking to each other, about their courses and assignments as well as non-academic things. But I am often surprised by how little students listen to each other in class – students who are models of attentiveness when the teacher is speaking. That is a mistake. As a course unfolds, you will begin to learn as much from your classmates as from your teachers, and by its climax you may well learn even more by that route. So:

- Listen hard to what everyone says in a class.
- Read each other's essays/assignments as regularly as possible.
- Quite often teachers ask you to work in pairs; extend that beyond the classroom if you can. Of course, there comes a time when you need to work entirely on your own, but using a fellow-student as a sounding-board beforehand can be highly productive. As your confidence increases, that relationship can even become (affectionately) adversarial, allowing you to test ideas in a stringent, enabling way.

Some of my best moments in the classroom have occurred when two or three students in effect take things over, becoming so involved in their discussions that I am practically irrelevant! When that happens, truly mature learning has become their norm, and it should be your goal regardless of subject or stage.

Instincts

A very short section, partly because the last few pages have implicitly signalled the need to be sharply focused as often as you can manage, and partly because the whole matter of instinct and intuition (including the 'hunch') is explored in Chapter 4. All I want to do here is encourage you to:

Trust the authority of your senses.

The remark was made many centuries ago by Thomas Aquinas, and it is a timeless truth. Your instincts are as much a part of your make-up as your powers of reasoning, and despite what many people claim, they are reliable much more often than not. Such 'trust' is not only a question of recognising fatigue, boredom or impatience; it also involves knowing when to ask, when to explore something in public and, equally, when to follow your own insights or ideas regardless. Yes, you will be wrong sometimes, as all of us are; however, staying in tune with how things strike you will prove as much a strength as taking full advantage of others' ideas, wisdom and guidance. No student is merely a brain, and the best students bring in *everything* to work for them.

Self-management III: scheduling

Another very short section – this time because I don't want to annoy you!

All students have it drummed into them till they're sick of it that:

Organisation and time-management are paramount.

Yes, all right, all right, all *right*. Just shut up, will you?

Students' irritation – which I entirely share – at this injunction is at least partially due to an implication that such things boil down to moral character. The idea is absurd, naturally. The issue is *a solely practical one*, and it is on that basis alone that I offer some brief observations.

Let's assume your desk is tidy, your equipment in good order, and that all you need is readily to hand. Let's also assume – it won't be true for all readers, but this should still help them – that you now have to plan your own private study slots rather than work from a day-by-day homework timetable provided for you. First tip:

Revisit that provision: construct your own day-by-day schedule.

This has two pluses. It gives an immediate shape to what will otherwise be a large and rather scary series of blanks. But unlike those earlier days:

You can change that daily schedule whenever you like and as often as you like.

You are now in the land of 'flexi-time'.[8]

Needless to say, you'll need to be aware of assignment deadlines and work to them; it's a good idea to build these into your schedule, maybe highlighted in some form. And you'll need also to log other non-study appointments and tasks you may have, including times devoted to recreation – which is my second tip:

Leave room in each week for 'fallow time' and off-duty *fun*.

While your scheduled list of assignments, assignations, the abundance of preparatory reading and so forth may soon seem pretty forbidding, that's better than having no idea when you're going to do what and how. That newly in charge flexibility should ensure that you manage. Your weekly rhythms and accomplishment of tasks will partly depend on the tough yet self-serving awareness of your bio-rhythms explored above, and you both need and can afford to take time off for rest and recreation. Self-knowledge is fundamental to your success, yes, but that does not include self-punishment!

Third and last tip:

As with your PC, don't let your personal schedule *dictate* to you.

You may now construct your own weekly timetable rather than have it pre-ordained, but it is still there to serve, not bully you. If you find yourself ignoring it 90 per cent of the time, then you need to do some serious thinking – including whether you should be doing this particular course in the first place, though given that you're aspirant high-flyers, that is unlikely to apply. And as I'll be exploring soon, you not only need time off but:

A once-a-day opportunity to 'chill out' completely.

Those occasions should be built into your study programme.

Self-management IV: comforts and pleasures

It is my impression that students – and their teachers – are much less puritanical about what constitutes a proper and successful working regime than was the case a generation ago. The notion that work must be done in silence and in a spartan, even uncomfortable environment has been largely discredited, and it is now broadly recognised that students tend to work best when they are comfortable and contented. Thus:

- If you want to work to music, do so.
- If you want a cup of coffee by you as you study, have it.
- When you feel yourself getting tired or find your attention wandering, have a short break.

You need to be honest and quite tough about all this even so. Don't choose music that drowns out your thoughts.[9] Don't get *so* comfortable that you quickly become drowsy. Don't allow your refreshments to distract or befuddle you.

Moreover, when it comes to your study-room, you should try to ensure that it quietly exudes the atmosphere of intellectual life. If you think that's pretentious, just think of the various class-rooms you inhabit each day. I'd be amazed if some weren't more attractive or welcoming than others, and I'd be hardly less surprised if you didn't find you work better in a classroom that seems designed for learning rather than one that has been recently adapted from being a broom cupboard or an aircraft hangar. Bring that 'comfort and appropriateness' into your own work space if you can: it will both relax and sharpen you.

Above all, try to regulate your aural environment. One of the reasons why the notion of working in absolute silence has become discredited is that absolute silence is almost impossible to find. Even in the most austere library there will be regular sounds; in a house or school there will be all sorts of noise, internal or external. These distract not because of their volume but because you have no control over them. That is, perhaps, the chief virtue of working to music, which not only (presumably) gives you plea-sure but also blots out nearly all such extraneous noise – a highly satisfactory combination.

In short and in sum, you want to aim at a state of affairs where:

Your working sessions coincide with your maximum levels of desire to work and power to do so.

One of the ways you can enable this is to make yourself as comfortable and serene as you can. As C.A. Mace put it seventy years and more ago:

Emotional temperance is needed for the pursuit of intellectual ends.[10]

His implicit emphasis on the importance of *pleasure* brings me to the last point in 'respecting the obvious' – the confirmatory:

All work and no play doesn't just make Jack a dull boy: it makes him a lousy student too.

The same goes for 'Jill', naturally. High-flyers, regardless of age or gender, put a lot of intense effort into their studies, and a lot of time too. That will be diluted and compromised if you don't look after your other needs and desires. You need recreation and fun, and you should act on that in a wholly guilt-free fashion.

So far, this chapter has considered and on occasion re-considered things which for all their importance are relatively straightforward and probably known to you. You might even think most of them are an obvious matter of common sense, and you'd be right. Now, however, we arrive at some things which are a good deal less than straightforward and where '*common sense*' does not apply.

GOING BEYOND THE OBVIOUS

Concentration

Only two things in life are certain: death and taxes

Benjamin Franklin's pronouncement has become one of the most celebrated of all quotations, but it is not entirely accurate. There is a third certainty: every student, at whatever time and in whatever place, has been told by an irritated or irate teacher to:

Come on now, *concentrate*!

Sometimes the rebuke is fair enough. But implicit in that command is the notion that *concentration* is a simple matter of 'getting a grip'. Or, to put it more formally and precisely, of:

Asserting your will to attend, your will to work.

That is not a simple matter at all: on the contrary, it is a highly complex, even slippery one. It is also fundamental, in that once you've understood some of the factors and phenomena which affect concentration, either positively or negatively, you'll already be much better organised, alert to what you need to do, when best to do it and how to cope when things suddenly go vague and dismal on you.

Students are apt to believe that if their 'will' is strong enough, they can force themselves to pay full attention and therefore to learn. While not entirely untrue – in certain cases and circumstances it undoubtedly applies – the idea is both dangerously simple and needlessly confrontational. By that I don't just, or even chiefly, mean a clash between student and teacher/mentor. My real concern is that:

It sets up a false confrontation within students themselves, whereby the will and the intellect become two combatants squaring up to each other.

That is the ideology of the boxing ring; not too many students have shone by battering into submission one or other determinant of their nature. Something a good deal more flexible and creative is needed, and it is to be found in the 'insatiable curiosity'[11] intrinsic to our species.

The more intelligent the student – and that means you! – the more eager s/he is to enquire, absorb and master things. The investigation which follows will, I hope, prove interesting in itself; more important, by the end of it you should understand how concentration is effected or lost, and how to apply that knowledge to your work patterns.

The will to work

This has five components:

Component	Focus
1 Specific goals (Content)	*What* we want to do
2 Intensity	*How much* we want to do
3 Times	*When* we want to work
4 Duration	*How long* we want to work
5 Polarity (between duty and pleasure)	Torn between feeling one *should* work and *not wishing to* at this particular juncture.

All five are *variable*. They all depend on energy-levels, desire, time of day and even such mundane but basic things as the weather and when you last ate or drank. And not only is it pretty clear that all such things both *impinge* upon *concentration* and are *affected by it*: it is equally clear, I think, that the problem of concentration is unlikely to be solved by voluntary effort or by an exertion of will. What is required instead is something more subtle and precisely focused – a careful organisation of conditions which jointly and variously control the

- direction
- time
- frequency of occurrence
- duration
- quality

of our study. And that means, above all, 'precise attention to detail' rather than relying on 'good old-fashioned hard work'.

When England won the Rugby Union World Cup in November 2003, manager Clive (now Sir Clive) Woodward was inevitably praised for his hard work and that of the squad – *all* of it, including the legion of back-up outfits. He did not exactly demur, but I noticed that instead of sheer 'industry' he kept stressing everyone's attention to detail. That was reflected in those back-up teams and in the years-long studies he made of everything that would allow the side to peak at the right time.

Yes, that was hard work all right. But it was a long way from the Protestant work ethic claim that diligence will automatically bring not only its own reward but many other garlands too. Woodward had no truck with that bogus doctrine: his kind of 'hard work' centred on being precisely, intelligently and vigorously focused at all times. That's how students get top grades too.

So with any task or project, look to be specific, not general; go for incisive detail, not blunt effort.

Don't say	Say instead
I must work harder at my Chemistry.	I must learn these twenty Atomic Table symbols by tomorrow evening.
I must improve my punctuation.	I will master the use of the apostrophe in the next hour.

I must improve my French grammar.	I will learn all the verbs that take *être* and not *avoir* in the perfect tense.
I must fully understand the relationship between Macbeth and his wife.	I shall study closely *Act I, Scene vii,* where their most intense and decisive conversation occurs.

Rhythm

I've discussed bio-rhythms and scheduling already, but these additional observations should further mobilise your will to work:

- Routines are highly desirable, but watch out for them becoming mere *ruts*. The latter are characterised by doing something for the sake of it or out of blind obedience to a timetable. Stay in tune and in charge.
- It has long been suggested that the afternoons are classically unfitted for mental work. You can't do anything about that in terms of class-time, but unless you are one of those quite unusual people whose brains are in top shape in the hours after lunch, take account of that phenomenon in planning your study time. Most academics find Spanish hours the most congenial – and if that includes 'siesta power-napping', go for it! A mid-afternoon snooze can do wonders for your evening energy.
- We all can suffer from loss of *inclination* rather than loss of *capacity*. This has been usefully called 'pseudo fatigue', but there's nothing bogus about its potentially damaging effects. To combat this:

1 Relax in some form every hour.
2 Take at least two or three hours off per day from work (not counting sleep).
3 Have one day of rest per week. (If you can: I know that for today's students, this desirable notion is very difficult to act on.)
4 Have one week off per two months.

All four are built into the school day/week/term, so it makes good sense to incorporate them in your private schedules.

Memory

This wonderful property is even more mysterious than concentration itself. However, the process by which we log something permanently in our memory can be reduced to a straightforward '3Rs' formula:

Reception   Retention   Recall

Further, there are also three ways in which material can be learned:

1   by repetition;
2   by the use of mnemonic devices;
3   by the perception of integrating relations/connections.

Those are the *only* three, by the way (discounting flukes). The third is arguably the strongest – mainly because the activity of relating things to other things and establishing links between superficially disparate material involves both repetition and the kind of 'creative play' that characterises all good mnemonics.

Further observations about memory and how best to go about Review and Revision are to be found in Chapter 6.

Challenge and self-confidence

One of the most notable characteristics of high-flying students is that they enjoy a challenge. Yes, they will sensibly take care of business when it comes to the routine stuff that is a staple part of any course, but it is the difficult (and therefore more interesting) tasks which attract them most. They tend to prefer demanding texts to easy ones, intricate theorems to standard formulae, complex and even semi-maddening problems to those that can be solved in a few minutes.

However, that will not *always* be your attitude or experience. Like all of us, you will have moments of frustration and self-doubt when something refuses to 'come out' or is insufficiently clear for you to proceed fluently or indeed at all. When that happens, do not let it prompt feelings of inferiority or any kind of despair. Instead:

1   have a rest or switch your attention to something else;

2   remind yourself that a fair amount of your work is *designed*
     to be demanding . . .
3   . . . and that if you don't find it so, you're not working
     properly.

That may seem a tortuous, even paradoxical way of cheering yourself up, but I assure you it will work. Self-confidence requires an
awareness of your gifts and strengths, but also an awareness of
what you don't yet know or cannot yet do. That *rational foundation* can be bolstered by adding a variant of something I
pinpointed in Chapter 2.

I spoke then of the enormous satisfaction one can derive from
proving your doubters wrong, be those Jeremiahs parents, teachers
or friends. Here the 'target' is not people but the material itself.
Your will to work will be invigorated by a healthy determination
not to let this stuff beat you, to show it who's boss. On occasion,
with younger pupils as well as senior ones, I will tell a class that I'm
not sure if they're going to be able to handle the task I'm setting
up. They invariably do! Apply that friendly goading to your private
struggles: such increased resolve will almost certainly pay off.

On, finally, to something which may seem 'obvious' but in
several crucial respects goes way 'beyond' that.

Punctuation and paragraphing

These techniques are a mixture of the elementary and the highly
sophisticated, and it is the latter which largely concerns me here.
I am not going to insult your intelligence by taking you through
a detailed survey of how, when and why you should use all the
punctuation points available or any such thing. I'm assuming
you're well versed in such rudimentary matters – which is why I
have not included anything on spelling or grammar either.[12] But
it is one thing to know in theoretical detail why punctuation is
used and how it works, quite another to *act* on that knowledge
at all times and in all circumstances.

Bright students who comfortably score full marks in a specific
punctuation exercise can prove much less reliable when punctu-
ating their own work. The reason for this is not hard to find. A
punctuation exercise is sharply and narrowly defined, and a good,
well-schooled brain reacts accordingly, focusing on what is a single
issue. In any piece of extended composition, however, several

preoccupations come into play, *and simultaneously.* That is perhaps most strikingly the case in a creative writing assignment, where you are required to:

- devise a narrative;
- structure it;
- create plausible characters, develop them;
- furnish them with dialogue which is conversationally authentic and narratively plausible/relevant;
- provide an ending that both works in its own terms and leaves the reader satisfied and/or still intrigued;
- obey a word limit, or at any rate keep an eye on your 'word clock';
- hand it in on time.

That is one hefty 'simultaneous' package, and if other projects are slightly less multiple in their requirements, all of them leave the student forgivably unfocused on such mundane things as where to put in the little flicks of the pen that orchestrate the prose, or where to give the reader essential respite in the form of paragraphs.

'Forgivably', maybe, but also damagingly, even disastrously. Take a critical look at these emails sent to me by a bright sixteen-year-old; apart from the name, which for obvious reasons I have changed, they read exactly as they appeared in my inbox.

> **Hello, Dr Richard palmer- you may not remeber me but my name is JOHN, i attended your class at the E Learning centre based on suceess in GCSEs. I found your class helpful and thankyou for your help. I was wondering if you could provide me with some advice. I wanted some advice on how to tackle a question on A View From The Bridge by Arthur Miller and Of Mice And Men by John Steinbeck also do you have any suggestion on what the questions might be, or who it might be based around? I will find it helpful to hear from you thankyou. Any advice would be helpful – thankyou.**

And here is his acknowledgement of the reply I sent:

**Thankyou for your advice dr palmer i am sorry for
the delay but i thank you i found the information
very helpful and hopefully it should help me to achive
a good grade. i welcome any further advice for GCSE
english. i thank you for your advice.**

As you may remember from Chapter 1, his strategic approach
is not one I would recommend; however, what most bothers me
here is the truly *awful* level of composition.

- The use of 'i' instead of 'I' is an early-primary-school illit-
  eracy.[13] In addition, he's not even consistent about it!
- The hit-and-miss approach to other capitalisations suggests
  that not only does he not know when to use them but has
  only the vaguest grasp of their purpose and function.
- The punctuation is erratic in letter number 1 and has got
  worse by number 2.
- There are at least four misspellings (including the illiterate
  compression of 'thank you') which are eloquent of hasty
  composition and zero editing.
- The expression is similarly frantic and unchecked. There are
  several repetitions, and at least two grammatical errors.
- His approach to sentence structure might be termed random,
  if you were in charitable mood: I'd call it non-existent.
- In sum and in short: there is an almost total absence of
  anything you could call considered thought.

I reckon I can hear you mouthing one of two responses (possibly
both) to that brutal appraisal:

1   Come on, it was only an email.
2   What a sad, nit-pickingly silly, nasty pedant!

My replies are:

1   Yes, *but* ...
2   No, *and* ...

My first response is that the notion that emailing reduces the
need for meticulous accuracy is to my mind false, lazy and
dangerous. However, it is not difficult to see how it arose and

why it has become so widespread a belief. Newcomers and veterans alike find email a highly pressured activity. Even when off-line and/or adding to other people's phone-bills rather than one's own, economic considerations seem paramount, willing the writer to get the job done as fast as possible. But in this case 'speed' is a decidedly double-edged property.

On the one hand, *speed* is undoubtedly electronic communication's chief virtue. It is now possible within the space of a morning for two parties to have a multiple exchange of letters on a call-and-response basis which explores and then settles a complicated matter – a process that might take a week if entrusted to 'snail mail'. Moreover, with email one knows – at once and almost invariably – whether your message has been received: no GPO uncertainty there! And extending our attention to Internet facilities, millions have found ordering goods or banking both faster and more efficient using this medium than former methods.

So far, so very good. But it is an important paradox that any virtue can become a vice; speed can become a major drawback if that property attends the email's actual composition and use of the 'send' button. Returning to that multiple exchange outlined above:

It will be *no good at all* if each letter is not clear and accurate.

Indeed, it will quickly multiply a whole lot more, in the form of irritated and tediously time-consuming enquiries:

- Why haven't you answered my chief question in email 1?
- I don't follow your paragraphs 2 or 4.
- What did your last letter *mean*, please?

and of course that 'old favourite':

- You haven't attached the promised attachment.

One of the most valuable mottos in existence is the Latin *festina lente*. Its literal translation, 'hurry slowly', translates into the timelessly wise oxymoron:

More haste, less speed.

Nowhere is that 'tag' more urgently relevant than in email practice. If it is not borne in mind, such communication can turn out to be slower than its 'ordinary' alternatives and very frustrating into the bargain.

And that may be just the start of your problems. Turning now to my second response, 'No, *and* . . .', the point is that:

Bad habits are notoriously catching.

I may strike you as a 'sad pedant' or worse in insisting that there is *never* a time when getting things right does not matter, but I have to say that you disagree at your peril. Sloppy email practice can soon spread into your more formal, considered writing. It is an insidious process, all the more dangerous for being invisible and indeed unconscious. Emailers who dispense with punctuation and other formal conventions will soon find themselves doing likewise in work that really does 'matter' – to *them*.

Actually, punctuation is *anything but a 'small thing'*. On the contrary, it is by some distance the most important 'basic skill' of them all.

- Bad spelling and faulty grammar are of course to be avoided, but unless they are ludicrously poor, they hamper rather than cripple: the reader can still follow what's being said.
- Bad punctuation *does* cripple, even destroy meaning. At best it leads to chronic ambiguity, at worst sheer senselessness. Moreover, deficient punctuation not only makes the reader's life a nightmare: it suggests a writer who isn't thinking or, perhaps, *cannot* think.

So whatever subjects you may be doing, ensure that your punctuation is *always* accurate and clear. For it dramatises two things fundamental to your success: the need to:

Build on rock, not on sand.

and the fact that:

The psychology of *writing* is – or should be – intimately connected with the psychology of *reading*.

Writers who do not bother to punctuate adequately show a blatant disregard for their readers' comfort. That is rarely their intention, naturally, but it is no less damaging for being unwitting. The need to bear your readers in mind is paramount whatever task you're doing, why you're doing it, and what its outcome might be.

That principle governs subtler matters too. It is remarkable how many dedicated professionals who are able communicators and writers fail to give any consideration to:

• when and by whom their document will be read;
• in what circumstances it might be read;
• at which point in an agenda it will occur;
• how much time it will take to read and/or will be spent on it; and so forth.

Such concerns may not seem directly relevant to students, who can be confident that their work will be read with detailed concentration; nevertheless, they point to the wisdom of bearing one's readers in mind at all times and, if you like, respecting their 'rights'. And another key area in which you will gain either their grateful approval or their irritated alienation is one that may be subtler and more sophisticated than basic punctuation but is hardly less important: *'paragraphing'*.

All English teachers – and a lot of other people too – put a premium on this skill for two main reasons:

1   Good paragraphing is an index of an organised mind and a clearly thought-out argument. It at once implies order, logic and control.[14]
2   Good paragraphing is 'user-friendly'. Even before readers start perusing the material, they are alerted to restful pauses awaiting them; such prose has an encouragingly comfortable 'look' about it.

That brings me to the phenomenon known as *'white space'*.

'Margins' are probably the aspect of white space that most people would cite first; while that provision is obviously important, it is not the most pressing – simply because it *is* obvious. Any writer who declines to furnish margins is either untrained or incompetent.[15]

However, even writers who are bomb-proof about margin-provision can get into major *white space* problems without realising it. Once they've shaped their overall design through the 'page set up' facility on their word processor or analogous long-hand means, they can then all too easily get carried away by the sheer intensity of composition, causing them to forget their readers almost entirely.

Bad provision of white space is intriguingly spectrum-like. At one end of the scale, there is the essay/document/article/letter that has *just too much of it* – paragraphs lasting a maximum of two sentences before the writer (implicitly) decides that the reader needs a good rest. That is patronising, stupid and simply wrong, despite the continued practice of tabloid newspapers and tabloid radio.[16]

At the other end of the scale, there is the writer who seems to have taken Green issues on board to an insane extent, regarding the use of a second or third sheet of paper as an environmental obscenity. The resultant prose is invariably close-spaced, small-fonted, under-paragraphed and in sum distinctly unpleasant to read even if the material is top-class. Yes, I know many of us get periodically angry about how many trees are pulped to produce utter rubbish[17] – but that phrase surely does not apply to your own academic work! So:

* Stop thinking that using paper sensibly is a crime.
* Choose a decent-sized font.[18]
* Go for '1.5 spacing', not 'single' or 'exactly'.

Put simply, good paragraphing and sensitive use of *white space* (including font-size) make a page look immediately attractive; failure to provide such 'comfort breaks' has the opposite effect. The following pages show examples of those extremes. The 'text' is taken from a piece you will encounter in full as a note-taking exercise in Chapter 5, 'Doing it'. Here I just want you to consider the effect of the four different layouts on your eye, concentration powers and general well-being.

White space: four contrasting layouts

I

The story of Elvis Presley is one that is not only both tragic and tacky but also decisively, almost symbolically, American. When he burst on the scene in the mid-1950s, Presley was a talent as shocking for some as he was exciting for others, full of a raw power whose sexuality was almost tangible. (Within months, any below-waist shots of Elvis performing were banned on US TV and newsreel.) He drew on the separate-yet-linked traditions of hillbilly music and the blues, a potent combination made all the more exciting by a voice at once true and husky and a rhythmic flair that no other mass-selling artist has ever approached. And to quote one of his 1958 hits, Elvis was 'Trouble'. In an America gripped by the Cold-War-dominated ethos of the Eisenhower years and for whom McCarthyism was still an issue, the youthful rebellion and sheer energy that Presley embodied were not only alarming but indecent to the point of un-Americanness. Marxism was, in Robert Hughes's phrase, 'America's nurturing enemy', and anything or anyone who diverted the nation's zeal from focusing on the 'Red Menace' was bad news – 'trouble' in abundance. Some readers may have an idea of what happened next. Presley remained a 'dangerous', youth-oriented singer for another two or so years, during which time he had an unbroken string of hits that mined further the earthiness of his first records, e.g. *Jailhouse Rock*, *I Got Stung*, *Big Hunk Of Love* and *Hard-Headed Woman*. Even while America's young was rocking and rolling to such joyous and seemingly anarchic sounds, though, a softening-up process was going on. Colonel Tom Parker,

Presley's manager, had already determined that Elvis would become an all-round family entertainer, for reasons that had as much to do with small-town conservative values as with money. In 1958 Presley went into the army. Unsurprisingly (it must now be said) he emerged as the model soldier, all modest dutifulness and artful (that is to say *coached*) gung-ho patriotism. By the time he was demobbed, middle – and *middle-aged* – America had already taken him to their hearts, and Parker's long-term plan streamrollered into action.

Why not use <u>this</u> white space more helpfully?!

I 350 words without a break in a size 10 font. Pity the poor reader!

II

The story of Elvis Presley is one that is not only both tragic and tacky but also decisively, almost symbolically, American.

When he burst on the scene in the mid-1950s, Presley was a talent as shocking for some as he was exciting for others, full of a raw power whose sexuality was almost tangible. (Within months, any below-waist shots of Elvis performing were banned on US TV and newsreel.)

He drew on the separate-yet-linked traditions of hillbilly music and the blues, a potent combination made all the more exciting by a voice at once true and husky and a rhythmic flair that no other mass-selling artist has ever approached. And to quote one of his 1958 hits, Elvis was 'Trouble'.

In an America gripped by the Cold-War-dominated ethos of the Eisenhower years and for whom McCarthyism was still an issue, the youthful rebellion and sheer energy that Presley embodied were not only alarming but indecent to the point of un-Americanness.

Marxism was, in Robert Hughes's phrase, 'America's nurturing enemy', and anything or anyone who diverted the nation's zeal from focusing on the 'Red Menace' was bad news – 'trouble' in abundance.

Some readers may have an idea of what happened next. Presley remained a 'dangerous', youth-oriented singer for another two or so years, during which time he had an unbroken string of hits that mined further the earthiness of his first records – e.g. *Jailhouse Rock, I Got Stung, Big Hunk Of Love* and *Hard-Headed Woman*.

Even while America's young was rocking and rolling to such joyous and seemingly anarchic sounds, though, a softening-up process was going on. Colonel Tom Parker, Presley's manager, had already determined that Elvis would become an all-round family entertainer, for reasons that had as much to do with small-town conservative values as with money. In 1958 Presley went into the army.

Unsurprisingly (it must now be said) he emerged as the model soldier, all modest dutifulness and artful (that is to say *coached*) gung-ho patriotism. By the time he was demobbed, middle – and *middle-aged* – America had already taken him to their hearts, and Parker's long-term plan streamrollered into action.

II An over-compensation. The font size (11) is better, but here there are far too many breaks and too much white space, creating a jerky rhythm injurious to prose-flow and reader-concentration.

III

The story of Elvis Presley is one that is not only both tragic and tacky but also decisively, almost symbolically, American.

When he burst on the scene in the mid-1950s, Presley was a talent as shocking for some as he was exciting for others, full of a raw power whose sexuality was almost tangible. (Within months, any below-waist shots of Elvis performing were banned on US TV and newsreel.) He drew on the separate-yet-linked traditions of hillbilly music and the blues, a potent combination made all the more exciting by a voice at once true and husky and a rhythmic flair that no other mass-selling artist has ever approached. And to quote one of his 1958 hits, Elvis was 'Trouble'. In an America gripped by the Cold-War-dominated ethos of the Eisenhower years and for whom McCarthyism was still an issue, the youthful rebellion and sheer energy that Presley embodied were not only alarming but indecent to the point of un-Americanness. Marxism was, in Robert Hughes's phrase, 'America's nurturing enemy', and anything or anyone who diverted the nation's zeal from focusing on the 'Red Menace' was bad news – 'trouble' in abundance.

Some of you may have an idea of what happened next. Presley remained a 'dangerous', youth-oriented singer for another two or so years, during which time he had an unbroken string of hits that mined further the earthiness of his first records – e.g. *Jailhouse Rock*, *I Got Stung*, *Big Hunk Of Love* and *Hard-Headed Woman*. Even while America's young was rocking and rolling to such joyous and seemingly anarchic sounds, though, a softening-up process was going on. Colonel Tom Parker, Presley's manager, had already determined that Elvis would become an all-round family entertainer, for reasons that had as much to do with small-town conservative values as with money. In 1958 Presley went into the army. Unsurprisingly (it must now be said) he emerged as the model soldier, all modest dutifulness and artful (that is to say *coached*) gung-ho patriotism. By the time he was demobbed, middle – and *middle-aged* – America had already taken him to their hearts, and Parker's long-term plan streamrollered into action.

III Considerably superior to I and II, but not yet quite right. The font is still too small for comfort, and while three 'breaks' over 350 words is often thought to be about 'par' as a paragraphing target, this is still pretty hard work.

IV

The story of Elvis Presley is one that is not only both tragic and tacky but also decisively, almost symbolically, American.

When he burst on the scene in the mid-1950s, Presley was a talent as shocking for some as he was exciting for others, full of a raw power whose sexuality was almost tangible. (Within months, any below-waist shots of Elvis performing were banned on US TV and newsreel.) He drew on the separate-yet-linked traditions of hillbilly music and the blues, a potent combination made all the more exciting by a voice at once true and husky and a rhythmic flair that no other mass-selling artist has ever approached.

And to quote one of his 1958 hits, Elvis was 'Trouble'. In an America gripped by the Cold-War-dominated ethos of the Eisenhower years and for whom McCarthyism was still an issue, the youthful rebellion and sheer energy that Presley embodied were not only alarming but indecent to the point of un-Americanness. Marxism was, in Robert Hughes's phrase, 'America's nurturing enemy', and anything or anyone who diverted the nation's zeal

from focusing on the 'Red Menace' was bad news –
'trouble' in abundance.

Some readers may have an idea of what happened next.
Presley remained a 'dangerous', youth-oriented singer
for another two or so years, during which time he had
an unbroken string of hits that mined further the earthiness of his first records, e.g. *Jailhouse Rock, I Got Stung,
Big Hunk Of Love* and *Hard-Headed Woman*. Even while
America's young was rocking and rolling to such joyous
and seemingly anarchic sounds, though, a softening-up
process was going on. Colonel Tom Parker, Presley's
manager, had already determined that Elvis would
become an all-round family entertainer, for reasons that
had as much to do with small-town conservative values
as with money.

In 1958 Presley went into the army. Unsurprisingly (it
must now be said) he emerged as the model soldier,
all modest dutifulness and artful (that is to say *coached*)
gung-ho patriotism. By the time he was demobbed,
middle – and *middle-aged* – America had already
taken him to their hearts, and Parker's long-term plan
streamrollered into action.

IV This may not be 'perfect', but it is, surely, the best of the
four. There are enough breaks to ensure reader-comfort
without risking condescension or stylistic fluency, and the more
generous font size (12) strengthens that user-friendliness.

Paragraphing: some guidelines

I would hope that you're now convinced of the governing importance in every kind of writing of *white space* and respecting your
reader. But within that ethos there are some 'writer-specific'
considerations which are worth investigating.

Earlier, I referred to paragraphing as a *skill*. Ultimately, it is
nothing of the sort: it is an *art*. Its good practice depends on feel,
'voice' and instinct rather than on any formula or techniques
which can dutifully be learnt. Conversely, and as we have seen,
its bad practice is often due to poor instinct or inadequate *feel*
rather than anything straightforwardly mechanical. Happily (if
somewhat paradoxically), instinct and feel can be substantially
improved by training and experience, so here are a number of
guidelines. They may not guarantee you perfect paragraphs every
time, but they should at least ensure that you will never paragraph
badly.

1   Each A4 sheet should usually contain two or three paragraphs.
2   Except on occasions when you wish to stress or highlight
    something, each paragraph should contain at least three
    sentences.
3   A good paragraph normally resembles a miniature chapter or
    essay: it should be clearly set up, properly developed, and then
    satisfyingly rounded off.
4   The first and last paragraphs of a piece should usually be
    fairly short.
5   A paragraph should have *unity*. You will probably ensure this
    by staying alert to point 3; in addition, you should always be
    wary of moving in mid-paragraph from one topic to another.
6   Try not to start a sentence until you're clear about how
    it's going to end. Important anyway, to adopt it as a regular
    discipline, will promote a much better 'feel' for when one
    paragraph should end and another begin.
7   Within reason, try to vary your sentence-length within each
    paragraph.

Staying alert to all seven and everything else I've explored should
put you in striking distance of Jonathan Swift's 'definition of a
style':

Proper words in proper places.

Punctuation and paragraphing: a cautionary tale

A friend of mine is the Chief Examiner in GCSE English for one of the major Boards. A little while ago he addressed a regional conference attended by a large number of Heads of English; at one point he was asked what he looked for in top-flight exam answers. I'm not sure what I was expecting him to say – something, perhaps, about flair, vigorous engagement with the material and clear evidence of individual response. Er, no. What he came out with was:

1   I look at the full stops. In the first place, *are* there any? And in the second, are they regularly and accurately deployed?
2   Then I look for paragraphs. Rather a forlorn quest in many instances.
3   And then I look at whether the end of the essay bears any relation to its beginning.

Those remarks were delivered with unimprovable dryness, and everyone laughed. Some of the laughter was incredulous; mine wasn't. One doesn't have to join ranks with the CBI and all those who moan about today's young lacking all basic skills to know that there are plenty of bright youngsters who are not entirely reliable in such matters. It is absurd to blame *them* for it, as many do. The fault lies in a National Curriculum which almost immediately abandoned its commitment to place grammar[19] at the heart of English syllabuses, and the consequent fact that many *teachers* are untrained in such things.

Be all that as it may, his triple answer may convince you that those unglamorous criteria are central to your high-flying aspirations. Even the most stunning architecture – physical or verbal – relies on sound foundations, just as the supremely-tuned body of a crack athlete is based on the known properties of bones and muscles. To repeat, as my last words on the subject, an earlier injunction:

Build on rock, not on sand.

Conclusion

Being both bright and ambitious, your self-management and organisational profile were in all probability already high before you started this chapter. But I hope you're now even better equipped and assured, properly aware of:

- When you work best and for how long.
- How to cope when needing to work at non-optimum times.
- The advantages of working to a timetable *you* have devised.
- The benefits of frequent and regular review.
- When to ask and also when to follow your own instincts and needs.
- The strengths and limitations of all your equpiment or 'kit'.
- The absolute importance of 'taking care of business' in terms of mechanical accuracy and keeping your reader contendedly with you.

I hope, too, that you're equally aware of these 'negative counterparts':

- It is unproductive to work when you are dog-tired.
- Never looking over your work from the moment it is finished until the exam looms is a recipe for ill-health, disaster, or both.
- Failing to ask for clarification when you don't understand something is the worst kind of foolish pride.
- Trying to second-guess the examiner who will assess you is a mug's game, wasting your time and distorting your energy.
- Omitting essential punctuation and paragraphing will not only cost you your readers' goodwill but is likely to ruin all that you're doing by rendering it incomprehensible.

As I've already observed, those principles seem governed by common sense. But although that term is not quite as unreliable as two related concepts we shall soon encounter, 'common knowledge' and 'common practice', it is still problematic. Any number of thinkers and doers bypass or ignore it every day, including students in their tens of thousands. That's why I headlined this chapter with Bill Larson's baleful observation about 'finding a cure for jerks'. Make sure you do not need one!

By now you should be fully versed in a number of things about study and about your own uniqueness as a student. You will be alert to the many pitfalls that lie in your path, the need to be toughly self-aware and well-organised and, most cheeringly, of the durable and indeed magnificent properties of your brain. But before we can go on to 'Doing it' and 'Making it', your foundations need to be complete, and that involves the need:

1   To sharpen up at *all* times the way in which you 'think'.
2   To distinguish, precisely, what you 'know' from what you *'believe'*, *'feel'* or can *'regurgitate'* according to the latest available information, study-pack, Internet guide or teacher.

That is our focus throughout the next chapter – 'Nailing it'.

Chapter 4

Nailing it

THINKING FOR FUN AND PROFIT

> Thought makes everything fit for use.
> Ralph Waldo Emerson

> Man is obviously made to think. It is his whole dignity and his whole merit.
>
> Pascal

You are now almost ready to perform as a high-quality writer and examinee. However, before it can be said that you're absolutely *in charge*, there is one more area we need to consider: the nature of 'knowledge' and indeed the whole activity of thinking.

What is knowledge?

The word 'philosophy' means 'a love of knowledge'. That includes an absorbed interest in determining how knowledge is imparted or deduced, in distinguishing between fact, opinion, prejudice and feeling, and in establishing precisely what we can (and cannot) know. An enjoyable activity for the intelligent anyway, it has the great additional benefit of sharpening the quality of one's thinking, critical response and arguing.

One of the best ways to improve – in any field – is to consider ways in which things went wrong or are flawed. So let us start by looking at three quite spectacular mis-prophecies by highly distinguished people, and then draw some conclusions from their mistakes:

'There is no likelihood that humans will ever tap the power of the atom.'	Nobel Laureate (Physics) Robert Millikan, 1923
'The Internet will never take off.'	Bill Gates, 1988
'I do not envisage a woman Prime Minister in my lifetime.'	Margaret Thatcher, early 1970s

These quotations show how precarious is any attempt to predict the future. For it is a simple but fundamental truth that:

Knowledge is necessarily and solely about and of the *past*.

Nobody can or ever has been able to *know* the future; anybody who claims otherwise is either a charlatan or mad. Note that:

The fact that many people *do* manage to predict events and occurrences more or less accurately or even exactly *does not prove that they knew what the future would bring*. Prophecy can often be impressive, even uncanny, but it is not *knowledge*.

We can go further. In *Heart of Darkness*, Joseph Conrad refers to 'destiny' as 'inscrutable', and the future itself is no less so.[1] Even the most brilliant, authoritative and informed people traffic in folly once they persuade themselves that the future is 'readable', for in the last analysis:

It is in the very nature of prediction to get things wrong.

Moreover, it is not just the future that cannot be *known*: neither can the present. By the time we have absorbed whatever may be at issue, it has become the past, however recent.

That is not to say that prediction, premonition and all analogous mental activity is without point or value. Far from it: at the end of this chapter I shall argue that our hunches and intuitions – not least our 'first impressions' – turn out to be surprisingly accurate surprisingly often, and that it is a great mistake to pooh-pooh them. But they are, clearly, a different matter from 'knowledge' when they actually occur. They may *become* 'knowledge', but only when we've had a chance to reflect on, test and ratify them – by which time we are analysing them as *past* phenomena.

However, dealing with knowledge is hardly less slippery for being a matter of history. Napoleon Bonaparte once asked, 'What is history but a fable agreed upon?', and while that might be an overstatement, you don't need to study history for very long, even at an elementary level, to realise how naive is the notion that it is bound solely by matters of fact and therefore objective. If that were so, historians themselves would never disagree, which of course they continually do. One of the more disputatious – and distinguished – was E.H. Carr:

> **The belief in a hard core of historical facts existing objectively and independently of the historian is a preposterous fallacy, but one which is very hard to eradicate.**[2]

He went on to observe that historians can be as selective about their facts as are diners about their food:

> **The facts are like fish swimming in a vast and murky ocean, and what the historian catches will depend partly on chance but mainly on what part of the ocean he chooses to fish in and what bait he chooses – these two facts of course being determined by the type of fish he wants to catch. By and large the historian will get the facts he wants.**[3]

That is not just a brilliant mixture of mischievousness and truth. It calls into question the very *reliability* of 'facts': perhaps they are every bit as slippery as knowledge itself. It might well be that another apparent overstatement, American novelist Norman Mailer's assertion:

> **Nothing is more difficult to discover than a simple fact.**[4]

will prove accurate. In any event, the matter requires immediate investigation.

Three angles on 'facts'

> Fact   **Accepted, observable or demonstrable truth.**
> **Facts must be supported by evidence; without it**
> **they can only be granted the status of opinion.**

That definition[5] was coined with primary schoolchildren and their teachers chiefly in mind, and on a 'square one' basis it is serviceable enough. Beyond that it won't do.

The opposition between fact and 'opinion' is much too simple. We have just been made aware, via E.H. Carr's analysis, that opinion and interpretation hinge on making the best possible use of available evidence – of choosing your facts to suit your argument. But the definition is additionally unsatisfactory in that all three governing adjectives are suspect.

That something is 'demonstrable' does not make it 'true'.

• For nearly 2,000 years a succession of highly intelligent and meticulous observers 'demonstrated' that the sun went round the earth, which was in addition flat and the centre of the universe.

• No less deluded, and a whole lot nastier, are such 'demonstrable truths' as medieval theology's view of woman as 'a failed man'[6] or the Nazis' 'proof' of Aryan superiority.

The other two, 'accepted' and 'observable', are more problematic still. We shall shortly see that the appeal to common knowledge – another term for accepted truth – is invariably precarious and often ridiculous, and also how fallible 'sensory observation' can be. Among all else, both those dangerously seductive concepts explain why humankind was deceived for over two millennia about the status, shape and behaviour of our planet.

So we need something much tougher and more penetrating, and that is provided by three sentences written 100 years ago by the first Professor of Psychology appointed by a UK university.

> **'Facts' themselves are not true. They simply *are*.**
> **Truth is the function of the beliefs that start and**
> **terminate among them.[7]**

Central to what any writer or thinker's life is about, those propositions are nonetheless very difficult, both to 'decode' and then to assimilate. However, they are absolutely of a piece with Carr's remarks in proposing that the real significance of facts – of all data, if you like – is how they are interpreted, how they are used by an individual, discerning human brain. That is how people arrive at the 'truths' which inform and direct their lives; it is also how they arrive at 'knowledge' as opposed to mere 'information'.

It is well worth remembering that the meaning of 'Science' as something distinct from 'the Humanities' or 'the Arts' is a pretty recent development. Until about 200 years ago it was simply another word for knowledge – unsurprisingly, since science comes from the Latin verb *scio*, meaning 'I know'. And it should be further borne in mind that the change in meaning does not signify the elevation of science into a 'safe truth', as many would and do assume it to be. That notion was stirringly challenged by a renowned mathematician and physicist a century ago:

> **Science is built with facts just as a house is built with bricks, but a collection of facts cannot be called a science any more than a pile of bricks can be called a house.**[8]

Like anything else, Science needs more than a database to be useful, let alone truly illuminating. That 'more' is human ingenuity and imagination – or to return us to this chapter's title and controlling concern, thinking.

What is truth?

This question is the most difficult ever asked. It was famously uttered by Pontius Pilate, who wisely 'did not wait for an answer': had he done so, he'd probably still be waiting as I write. William James's answer analysed above is a very good one, but it still doesn't solve the problem to everyone's satisfaction, or maybe *anyone*'s. The reason for that can be found in another simple but fundamental sentence:

> **How much of what you know is true?**

Here is a 'mini-quiz' to set you on your way.

1   Identify something you have been told which you believed at
     the time but now know to be false. How did you find out
     the truth?
2   Think of something which you are sure you *know*. Does
     anyone else know it too?

If my experience is any guide, an overwhelming majority of
you will have replied to question 1 with 'Belief in Father Christmas/
Santa Claus'. It is no less telling an example for being so popular,
and you might be amused by this brief gloss on the subject:

> **if small children believe that Father Christmas and the
> Tooth Fairy really exist, why spoil their pleasure?
> Most parents would probably agree, but they might
> begin to worry if a child reached the age of sixteen
> and remained convinced that Santa comes down the
> chimney on 24 December.[9]**

Two more sombre examples might be the 'Weapons of Mass
Destruction' affair attending the USA–UK's 2003 war with Iraq
and its considerable aftermath, or the hindsight that rationalises
a failed love affair, especially if its end was bitter. I shall return
to that latter paradigm later.[10]
     When it comes to question 2, the commonest responses hinge
on 'love' or 'faith'. You can *know* to the depths of your being
that you love your wife/husband/partner/mother/father/God, but
you cannot *prove* it to anyone else or indeed to the figure in question: not even sacrificing your life in the cause would be definitive
or beyond dispute.[11]
     Whatever your answers may have been, we can proceed to three
questions crucial to any advanced programme of study:

3   When and how do you know if something is true?
4   To what extent, and how, is truth 'relative'?
5   Which of the subjects that you're studying is the most
     'reliable', and why?

Question 3 admits of such a multiplicity of answers that I shall
not venture any 'representative' examples. The real point – as with
so many things to do with study and indeed life itself – is that

it's up to *you* to decide why you hold something to be true, and to test that decision as rigorously as you can.

Question 4 is, I admit, very annoying, being both huge and, on one level, pointless, since all human knowledge is *provisional*. It is also *incremental*: as a species we know far more than we did a generation, let alone three centuries, ago and our counterparts in a further 300 years will doubtless be staggered by our ignorance. But this question is nevertheless useful in leading us to a set of important distinctions:

A   There are things which are true now.
B   There are things which are true now but once were not.
C   There are things which were true once but no longer.
D   There are things which were never true.

Can you identify which one of the four applies to the following statements? My commentary follows immediately afterwards.

		A, B, C or D?
1	Elvis Presley is alive.	
2	The earth is flat.	
3	Tony Blair is the British Prime Minister.	
4	Hawaii is one of fifty states which make up the United States of America, an independent Republic.	
5	English is a compulsory subject for all UK schoolchildren up to the age of 16.	
6	England is a monarchy	
7	The atom is the smallest form of matter.	
8	Human existence is dependent on water.	
9	Nature is benevolent.	

Commentary		
1	**C**	No longer true, whatever the legion of 'Elvis Lives!' loonies may say! Obviously, however, it was true in, say, 1960.
2	**D**	Always untrue, no matter how many people believe it and how long the falsity took to be revealed.
3	**B** (or C)	True as I write; by the time this book is published, however, it may not be. And if students are still reading these pages in twenty years' time, it *certainly* won't be.
4	**B** (x 2)	A double whammy! Hawaii became an American state in 1959; until 1776 America was a British colony.
5	**B**	The temptation is to nominate **A**, since it's such a central fact of current student life. Yet 'English' only became a recognised university discipline in the early twentieth century, and that was reflected in school terminology too. Children of that era may have studied 'Reading and Writing', but the activity was not termed 'English'; in addition, it was not until 1974 that children were required to attend school to the age of 16.
6	**B**	It wasn't a monarchy between 1649 and 1660.
7	**C** or **D**	The atom was split in the 1920s, hence the **C**. However, it might be argued that since that operation was successful, it was never true that the atom was the smallest unit of matter. Like statement 2, it was a falsity waiting to be exposed. So **D** is the better choice.
8	**A**	Not only true now but one of the few things I can think of which has always been true.
9	**D**	Nature has no consciousness, conscience, or any ethical framework whatever: nature just is. Note that the antithetical proposition 'Nature is malevolent' would be equally (and always) untrue. As Professor Richard Dawkins tersely puts it: 'Nature is neither kind nor unkind.'[12]

Finally, concerning the question (no. 5) which asked you to nominate the most 'reliable' of your subjects, I would hope that you're already very wary about that adjective. In the exercise just covered, only one – no. 8 – of the nine statements proved truly 'reliable', and earlier we saw that those supposedly 'objective' disciplines, History and Science, are much more a matter of interpretation and opinion than might initially be imagined.

The same caution is needed when appraising *any and all subjects*. Furthermore, you need to be careful that you don't confuse the descriptor 'reliable' with your 'preference' for this subject or that. If you are very good at Discipline *x* and much less strong on Discipline y, there is a powerful temptation to think that *x* is 'sounder' than *y*. Not so, of course:

Aptitude + Attendant Affection is a potent and most welcome mixture, but it says much more about *you* than about the subject's intrinsic properties, *'reliability'* included.

So much for now about the subjectivity of truth, reliability and the eternally vexed question of what constitutes fact or where that leads us. It is now time to look at *kinds* of knowledge – an investigation that will require you to answer a host of questions even more challenging than the ones you've answered thus far.

What *types* of knowledge are there?

It has been persuasively suggested that there are just three types of question.[13]

I Questions which have one correct answer

Put simply but soundly, such questions hinge on matters of fact. The chemical formula for water is H_2O, not X_4H; the author of *Middlemarch* is George Eliot, not T.S. Eliot or Ferdinand McTosswit; one of the most influential but tyrannical figures of the twentieth century was Lenin, not (John) Lennon.

All quizzes – from *Mastermind* to a pub evening in Middlewallop or wherever – traffic solely in such questions. Any quiz that even vaguely embraced the criteria discussed under sections 2 and 3 below would be impossible. It would last forever, or until such time as everyone got so fed up that they went home not knowing who (if anybody) might win the wretched quiz before death intervened – not a great recipe for a fun evening out.

Those remarks do not indicate a flippant attitide to basic matters of provable information; as I've been at pains to emphasise throughout, all knowledge is based on recorded and safe *data*. But the real point is that while such information is the 'foundation' of knowledge, it emphatically is not the whole 'building'. Otherwise, *Mastermind* would incontravertibly mean what its title implies – that the ability to answer correctly thirty-five factually checkable questions means you are a great thinker. Once again, and obviously: not so.

2 Questions that have many possible answers but which require justification and reasoned judgements

Two examples:

- What is the best way – is there indeed *any* way – to tackle the Middle East situation?
- How can we ensure that our children have a healthy and safe diet?

Any number of possible solutions can be advanced to either question. Some may be transparently inadequate; more than a few are likely to be cogent and worth taking seriously.

However, such richness of sound alternatives can itself create a problem: how does one choose which might be the most effective? That is hard enough for an individual; it is much more difficult for a committee. Perhaps that's why so many obviously urgent problems take so long to be put right despite the concentrated good will of all concerned.

3 Questions that have no correct answer but depend solely on the person answering

An example might be, 'Which brand of cola tastes best?' My choice of 'taste' is deliberate, for answers to an enormous number of questions are, finally, a matter of nothing else. 'Taste' is definingly personal and almost entirely subjective, whether it be literal or metaphorical, as in all aesthetic matters.[14] You can disagree profoundly with others' taste, you can even find them guilty of bad or appalling taste, but very rare are the times when you could call them *wrong*.

Any Advanced student is going to encounter probably thousands of questions of each type. One of the secrets of successful study and enquiry is to know the difference between them, and any others you might think of. Here's a quite challenging exercise to help sharpen that awareness.

Into which of the three categories do these questions fit? You are not confined to a single choice, for you may decide that a number of them admit of two or more possibilities. You may also decide that you need further options, identifying a Type 4 or even 5.

		1, 2 or 3?
1	Which is the largest country in the world?	
2	Who is the British minister with responsibility for education?	
3	When was the First World War?	
4	Is it wrong to kill?	
5	What colour are your eyes?	
6	What colour is grass?	
7	Does God exist?	
8	Are we God's creatures?	
9	Are you well?	
10	Is your teacher well?	
11	Is two plus two always four?	
12	Does violence on TV contribute to violence in the community?	

		1, 2 or 3?
13	Does rampantly irresponsible sex on TV contribute to rampantly irresponsible sex in the community?	
14	Do extremely boring documentaries, make-over and gardening programmes contribute to the growing suicide rate?	
15	Was Hitler a good leader?	
16	Can a male doctor know more about childbirth than a mother of ten children?	

That's quite a range of questions. Some will have interested or engaged you more than others; some will have seemed easy, others very difficult; one or two may have struck you as just silly. But in general – and this is the crucial point – they are much more debatable than might first appear. See how your responses compare with mine.

Commentary		
	Type	Justification/Explanation
1	1 & 2	Apparently a simple 1: the answer is 'Canada'. But since the question does not specify whether 'largest' is a matter of area or population, it could equally be regarded as a 2. And in view of our earlier focus on the 'relativity' of truth, it's worth recalling that until the early 1990s the correct answer would have been USSR.
2	2	The question is not precise enough, and could be seen as fundamentally flawed. There are several ministers responsible for education under our current governmental system: moreover, it could be argued that the ultimate responsibility for the matter lies with the Prime Minister.

	Type	*Justification/Explanation*
3	**1 & 2**	The simple answer is '1914–18'. But many would say it's too simple, ignoring the fact that in some respects the war continued beyond the 11 November Armistice. And while the first military engagements may have been in September 1914, those (literally) millions of people interested in the origins of the war might well argue that such a 'fact' is no more than a 'local statistic', the inevitable outcome not only of the assassination of Archduke Ferdinand in Sarajevo but of a process that had been evolving for a very considerable time.
4	**3**	The question is absurdly vague for all its instant emotional impact. Kill what? Loved ones? Enemy soldiers? Armed would-be assailants? Cattle for human consumption? Fish ditto? Plants ditto? Flies?
5	**1 or 2**	For something so basic to nearly all humans, 'colour' is a maddeningly elusive concept. Many eyes are a subtle mixture of colours; even someone with unambiguously blue eyes might prompt debate as to whether they were sky-blue, carnation-blue, watery blue and so forth.
6	**2 or 3**	Not **1**. Arguably the most stupid simile in English is 'as green as grass': there are probably over a hundred different shades of green that grass can have, dependent on time of year, locale and many other things. And of course a lot of grass isn't green at all: there aren't many colours it can't be or hasn't been.
7	**2, 3 or 4**	Again, not **1**: no human can prove the existence of God (or his non-existence either). Initially I thought this a **2**; then, given that the issue is so much a matter of unique personal reflection, I tended towards **3** instead. But finally it occurred to me that the question is impossible to answer, which is my definition of **Type 4**. Note that, intriguingly, if the question were to be rephrased as 'Does the idea of God exist?', the answer would be a cast-iron **1**.

8	**As for 7**	All adjustments duly made, the same remarks apply here as immediately above. If forced to choose, I'd go for **4**.
9	**1 or 3**	If you take it to mean a routine enquiry about whether you're ill or not, **1**. If you dwell even briefly on the various possibilities signalled by 'well', it's a **3**.
10	**4**	The question is unanswerable by anyone other than the subject himself/herself. Even then it's problematic, as the second part of my commentary on no. 9 suggests.
11	**1 or 2**	Most of us would plump for **1**, and with certainty. But some very good mathematicians of my acquaintance are less confident, so maybe we should all be cautious!
12	**2 or 4**	Certainly not the **1** that many believe it to be, but it can't really qualify as a **3** since there are only two possible answers, 'yes' or 'no'. However, I would personally say that it's impossible to answer to any satisfying degree: if 'yes', to what extent?/how directly? and so forth. The proposed relation between cause and effect is so tenuous as to be either meaningless or unrecordable, so this is a **4**.
13	**2 or 4**	This is essentially a spoof of the above. But it is not entirely facetious, for it underlines how suspect is the understanding of cause and effect that characterises wholly earnest questions like no. 12.[15]
14	**5**	**5** denotes a very silly question/one not worth asking. I hope this made you smile, but it has no value – or even status – as an argument.
15	**1 or 2**	Depends who you are and where you stand. The obvious answer is 'No' on a **1** basis, but it would not just be bigots or lunatics who would opt for **2**.
16	**2**	This question hinges on what precisely you take 'childbirth' to signify. If you understand it as 'the physical experience of giving birth', then the answer is of course 'No'. But if you read it as 'the science of obstetrics', then the answer will almost certainly be 'Yes'.

It is surely significant that not one of those answers is an unam-
biguous 1, and that even as an *arguable* type, 1 applies in under
half the sixteen specimens. The exercise would appear to confirm
just how rare is Norman Mailer's 'simple fact'; it also points to
the superiority of vigorous investigation over dutiful acceptance.
To put it another way, it shows the value of 'critical thinking'.

That has been my aim almost from the start. I must emphasise
that the term does not necessarily imply disparagement: much
great 'criticism' centres on admiration and celebration, not fault-
finding or disapproval. That said and meant, we now take a
detailed look at 'fallacious arguing', reactivating my belief that a
very good way to improve your own performance is to examine
errors by others.

Common fallacies/disreputable or specious arguing

'Fallacy' comes from the Latin verb *fallior* ('to fail, to err, to be
mistaken') and it denotes an argument that, however plausible or
superficially impressive, is at best logically invalid and at worst
meaningless, even absurd.

Fallacious arguing comes in many forms and serves any number
of hidden agendas. Fifteen terms are investigated in this section.
Some of them – identified by a * – are self-explanatory, but the
majority of them require some kind of brief explanation or 'translation', which I have duly provided, along with three examples of
each type. Some of those are irreverent, and I hope they amuse;
none of them, however, is in any sense frivolous. Some of the
silliest arguing in human history has carried inexplicable weight
and credibility, and any such instances require gleeful mockery as
a matter of duty.

I   Hasty generalisation

I've started with this for two reasons. First, it is probably the most
well-known form of faulty arguing and also the most frequently
perpetrated. Second, quite a few of the other types which follow
also qualify as *hasty generalisations*.

Nearly all generalisations are suspect in some way. *Hasty* generalisations are those which are evidently absurd, even if all of us
are guilty of the practice at some time or another!

1   Dai stole my wallet. All Welshmen are thieves.
2   Most of my friends don't like the sitting MP, so he won't be
    re-elected.
3   All the one-day-internationals I've attended have been enor-
    mously exciting: this one is going to be just as good and just
    as close.[16]

2   Ad misericordiam

An argument that appeals only to pity or mercy.

1   We hope you'll accept our recommendations. We spent the
    last twelve weeks working extra time on them and we are
    quite exhausted.
2   Please give me a good grade – my parents will be furious if
    I don't get one.[17]
3   You *always* win when we play tennis. Can't you let me win
    just this once?

3   Ad hominem

An argument directed to or at the individual or the personal;
invariably it appeals to *feeling*, not *reason*.

1   You argue that God doesn't exist, but that's simply because
    you're so unimaginative.
2   Kevin's analysis of his ex-wife should be ignored because he
    is very bitter about her.
3   Why should we listen to your observations about Tim's unsuit-
    ability? You just want the job yourself.

4   *Unpalatable consequences**

1   I'm not going to believe Sarah's story about David because I
    couldn't stay with him if it were true.
2   You must believe in the rule of law, otherwise we'd all become
    savages.
3   God has to exist, or life would have no meaning.

5   *Appeal to authority*

This has its roots in the medieval concept of *auctoritas*, which
boils down to the idea that if it is written in manuscript form, it

is true. At that time, only clerics, i.e. Churchmen, and a few excep-
tional individuals had access to the written word; that naturally
gave them immense power/'authority', for both good and ill.

It would be very unwise to be snootily condescending about the
pre-printing-press beliefs of 600 years ago and more. The idea that
the written word has incontrovertible authority or rightness has
survived to this day, and virulently. We continue to use such idioms
as 'playing it by the book' and 'brought to book'; in addition, just
think of the several hundred 'bookings' which occur during a week-
end of professional football. It can also be detected in those millions
of gullible souls who *still* think that the printed word is automatically true or that the Internet is by definition reliable.

1   One of the world's top bankers states that house prices will
    fall soon.
2   Last year's Nobel Laureate for Literature says that Western
    educational methods are fundamentally unsound.
3   It must be true – this book says so!

6   Loaded language*

1   Sensible people will agree with me that a referendum on the
    euro is essential.
2   This brilliant initiative will not appeal to dull minds.
3   QCA *claims* that educational standards continue to rise.

7   Appeal to common practice

1   Some people say that buying coursework essays off the
    Internet is cheating, but most people do it, so it's okay.
2   We've always done it like this, so it must be right.
3   Corruption in big business is a fact of life: there's no point
    worrying or trying to do anything about it.

This highly unreliable appeal has a cousin – the recourse to
'common knowledge'. The noun is rarely justified, which in turn
reduces the adjective to its most forlorn meaning – 'lacking in all
quality, taste or sense'. It is remarkable how many times the clause
'It is a well-known fact that . . .' precedes an assertion that is
neither well-known nor a fact,[18] and such common knowledge
myths as these are similarly lacking in foundation:

- Women are more emotional than men.
- Black people are indigenously more athletic than other racial types.
- Girls work harder than boys.
- Dogs are more friendly than cats.[19]

8   Red herring

An alternative term would be *non sequitur* – that which does not follow and is, therefore, irrelevant.

1   The Channel Tunnel runs at a loss only because of interest payments on the original loans; besides, most of the banks owed money are Japanese.
2   Only women are entitled to an opinion about breast 'versus' bottle-feeding; to allow men to get involved in the matter is yet another instance of the age-old male oppression of women.
3   I may be Railtrack's Chief Executive but I happen to prefer travelling by car.

9   Zero relevance

Of course, *all* fallacious arguing is deficient in value, but there are two types which qualify in particular.

Here are three examples of what is sometimes termed 'spurious conflation' or, more graphically, 'straw man stupidity' (after the character in *The Wizard of Oz* whose defining lament was 'If I only had a brain').

1   I can't understand anyone wanting to cut military expenditure. Why would anyone want to leave our country defenceless?
2   You can't identify 'joy' as a physical phenomenon, so it's a delusion.
3   If exam results improve, standards must be rising.

Superficially powerful, those assertions do not actually make sense. The perpetrators may not normally be brainless, but on this occasion they simply weren't thinking straight.

The next three propositions are likewise superficially impressive; they are also equally valueless, though for a different reason.

1   You cannot explain where God is, so God doesn't exist.
2   Scientists have not proved that global warming will occur, so there is no point in addressing the matter.
3   We do not know for sure how the cosmos was created, so the account in *Genesis* has as much weight as Darwin's.

Such arguing is sometimes (rather pompously) called *ad ignorantiam*: the 'ignorance' signalled does not indicate 'lack of information or knowledge' but that absolute condition, 'unknowability'. The limitations of human perception and knowledge mean that there are things about which we cannot usefully comment. The three examples given may command initial respect due to the sheer scale of the ideas in question, but only a few moments' reflection is required to see that it is precisely that conceptual magnitude which renders all three meaningless.

10   False dilemma*

1   You're either for us or against us.
2   America: love it or leave it.
3   Either we retain the pound as our currency or we sacrifice all national sovereignty: that is the choice before us.

11   Ad bacculam

An argument based on threat or menace. An easier and more or less analogous term might be 'moral blackmail'.

1   You'd better endorse the company's policy on positive discrimination or you'll be out of a job.
2   The defendant must be innocent because if he isn't there will be an uncontrollable riot.
3   If you do not recognise the true God you will face eternal damnation.

12   Contradiction in terms*

1   Everything I say is a lie.
2   It is impossible for the written word to communicate anything.
3   Buy three and save money.

13   Circular arguments

This particular fallacy is more often called 'begging the question'. Perhaps unreasonably, I've always detested the phrase, which combines pomposity and obscurity to a singular extent. Whichever term one uses, it denotes *the assumption of something which as much needs to be proved as your assertion*. My favourite 'circular argument' is the delightful 'If we had some bacon we could have bacon and eggs if we had some eggs'. The three arguments below are less ludicrous but just as flawed; you may even find numbers 1 and 2 faintly sinister in their erroneousness.

1   Capital punishment is necessary because without it murders increase.
2   Fox hunting is entirely defensible because the fox enjoys the chase.
3   God exists because the Bible says that he does, and the Bible is God's own truth.

14   False cause

1   On both occasions when I crashed my car I was wearing that shirt. I'll never wear it again.
2   Obese students get bad exam grades; you'd better go on a diet if you want to go to university.
3   Their marriage was bound to fail – hence their divorce last week.

Number 3 is an example of the fallacy known as *post hoc, ergo propter hoc*. Almost all my students have found this term and concept difficult, and rightly so. I hope devoting a discrete section to it will assist understanding.

15   Post hoc, ergo propter hoc

The Latin translates as 'after this, therefore because of this' – which is of marginal use unless you already understand the concept anyway! It signifies a 'false chronology': on a simplistic level, something approximating 'Because *x* happened, it was always *bound* to happen.' While sound, however, that doesn't tell the full story. What is also involved is a confusion of 'intention' with 'result', or if you like, a grafting of *the eventual outcome* onto the *original situation/set-up,* so that the two corruptedly become synonymous or indeed identical.

On Saturday, 7 October 2004, England played Wales at Old Trafford in a World Cup Qualifier and won 2–0. The second goal was scored late in the game by David Beckham – a marvellous 25-yard shot which fizzed into the top corner. Shortly afterwards he clashed with Welsh defender Ben Thatcher going for a 50–50 ball; he clearly suffered some kind of rib injury as a result. A few minutes later he rashly clattered into Thatcher and was shown the yellow card. It was his second booking of the tournament thus far, and that meant he would be suspended from England's next match. Shortly afterwards he left the field to have his injury attended to fully.

What happened next dominated the papers – and not just the sports pages – for some time. A few hours later Beckham claimed that he had *deliberately* got himself booked: he had at once known that his rib injury was bad enough to keep him out of the next fixture, and he thought it a smart move to be suspended for a game he'd miss anyway, since it would 'wipe his slate clean' for the remainder of the tournament.

A lot of people did not credit Beckham's story, including all those who don't believe he is clever enough to think up such a ruse. They argued that he would not have been able to diagnose his injury with such certainty in the heat of the moment (and the heat of his pain), that his challenge on Thatcher was just another instance of the arrogant petulance which has dogged him for years, and that his story was a smart-alec attempt at damage limitation which did not work. On the other hand, a number of other observers took the story at face value, accepting it as a true account.

That populous tribe bored stiff by football will not be alone in labelling the episode a thoroughly trivial one. But I've cited it because of its twofold *academic* significance:

- The truth or facts are most unlikely to emerge decisively.
- For anyone to any degree sceptical about it, Beckham's story is a classic instance of *post hoc, ergo propter hoc.*

His post-match argument states that his booking was not just the outcome of his reckless challenge on Thatcher but its original intention.

To put it in grammatical terms, his behaviour either describes an adverb clause of result:

A   Beckham was so determined to foul Thatcher *that he was booked and suspended from the next game.*

or one of 'purpose':

B   Beckham was determined to foul Thatcher *so that his suspension would be served while he was injured.*

If you believe his story, you're in the 'B' camp; if you don't, then your 'A' option also signals your suspicion that Beckham has trafficked in '*after this, therefore because of this*' smoke-screening.

Before we leave this topic, let us briefly return to a scenario outlined earlier – 'the hindsight that rationalises a failed love affair' – and investigate it further as a potential case of *post hoc, ergo propter hoc.*

> When A realises that B no longer loves A, especially if B is now seeing C, there is a stong temptation on A's part to dismiss B as fickle, flighty or just worthless. In an attempt to salvage something from the painful wreck, A reflects, 'I'm well out of it. B never loved me from the start. I'm going to look for an honest D.'[20]

Among all else, that little tale is the basis of upwards of 10,000 pop songs over the last fifty years. It is rather sobering to reflect that in nearly all instances such a thought process is, however understandable and appealing, *just not true.* Because it all went wrong and B is unfaithfully seeing C does not mean that B never loved A or was always looking for a C. Of course, that is *possible*; but it does not follow *automatically* – and that is what a *post hoc, ergo propter hoc* argument asks you to swallow, whether the motivation is cynical (Beckham, if you're an unbeliever) or innocent (poor old A).

Having spent quite a while on inadequate arguing and how to avoid it, it's time to accentuate the positive.

Justifying your thinking I: good reasons

The uniquely human activity of '*reasoning*' seems straightforward enough, signifying the capacity 'to think in a logical and controlled fashion'. Yet the 'reasons' we have for thinking as we do are *multiple*; in addition, they are not all the product of what can properly be called *reasoning*. That does not make them invalid or even inferior, but it does, evidently, make them different. And since committed students are going to spend a fair proportion of their time arguing a host of cases across several separate subjects, it is important to be aware of the disparate *'types of reason'* that we have, how they work and when they best apply.

Below are twelve things which (for the purposes of this exercise) I shall claim to know, accompanied by the type of reason it uses. My commentary will follow, but as you peruse the list, are there any 'matches' which you consider questionable? Are there, also, any claims which could admit of more than one reason? And can you think of any further types?

	I know . . .	Type of reason
1	The grass is green because I can see it.	Sense perception
2	3 × 3 = 9.	Logic
3	I have a fear of lightning.	Self-awareness
4	I played squash yesterday.	Memory
5	What the scientist said was true.	Authority
6	Women are more emotional than men.	Common knowledge
7	Exactly what God wants of me.	Revelation
8	That my redeemer liveth.	Faith
9	Beethoven is superior to the Beatles.	Value judgement
10	I love my father.	Instinct
11	It is wicked to murder a person.	Intuition
12	It will rain tomorrow.	Hunch

Commentary

1   Sense perception

I've already commented on the linguistic poverty of 'as green as grass', and soon we shall also be taking a look at how our senses can deceive us. Those two reservations duly expressed, no. 1 could not be defined as anything other than 'sense perception'. I suppose it could be wittily argued that the reason in question is 'memory' or faith or even common knowledge, but diverting though the discussion might be for a while, none of them stands up.

2   Logic

Again, no contest. A couple of high-class mathematicians of my acquaintance have suggested that accepting '3 × 3 = 9' hinges on 'authority', memory or faith, but they were not entirely serious. Of course, what constitutes a number, the relations between numbers and also the status of the symbol '=' are all problematic,[21] but those considerations do not affect the status of no. 2 as a logical deduction.

3   Self-awareness

I can see why you might opt for 'instinct' here. Any *phobia* is by definition irrational, whereas 'self-awareness' implies careful, honest reasoning. But here the latter is the better choice precisely because of that: phobia it may be, but its existence has been absorbed and understood.

4   Memory

An easy one. Needless to say, the memory can play tricks, and the statement may turn out to be wrong. However, that would not alter the reason underpinning the remark.

5   Authority

The belief in someone's authority is of course a form of faith, and if you plumped for that here nobody could quarrel with you. However, a more or less unquestioning acceptance of expertise is a peculiar *kind* of faith, which admits of many things. Number 8 could not be considered a matter of authority, could it?

Incidentally, it is not remotely clear from this remark whether 'the scientist' has 'said' something about science: the 'what' could be *anything*! The appeal to or use of authority always needs to be weighed with great care.

6   Common knowledge

I've already commented sufficiently on both the proposition and the concept itself. But however flawed and indeed absurd such instances are, it is a reason we all of us use at some time or another, and therefore needs to be taken good note of, if only for purposes of avoidance.

7   Revelation

All sorts of things might seem to underscore or prompt this or similar 'revelations' – acute self-awareness; faith; 'intuition'; even a 'hunch'. But the idea of *mysterious visitation* central to revelation transcends all those, and that is surely the governing idea here.

8   Faith

The only real contender, ultimately. Such a belief could be accompanied or prompted by revelation, yes; but that is not essential for the belief to be an unswerving and certain one. Please note that such certainty cannot be called knowledge. However much a devout believer might assert it as such, this is something which *cannot be known*: that, after all, is the whole point about faith and indeed its defining property.

9   Value judgement

We indulge in these all the time. There is no harm in that, nor any call to despise this reason as a mere opinionatedness. Our tastes and views are fundamental to us as unique individuals who think, feel and believe, and it would be idiotic to 'downgrade' them simply because they can never aspire to 'factual' status. The key to 'value judgement' is to be aware that it is just that, however much it may incidentally impress as 'authoritative', apparently 'logical' or even on occasion 'revelatory'.

10–12   Instinct, intuition and hunch

I've bracketed these together because:

a   They seem – and in some respects *are* – semi-synonymous, as these *OED* extracts demonstrate:

    1   Acting on *instinct* is 'to act without conscious decision'.
    2   To *intuit* is 'to know immediately without reasoning'.
    3   A *hunch* is 'a hint; an intuitive feeling'.

b   They are all seriously problematic as 'modes of knowing',
     being both very difficult to explain and therefore to justify.
     As a result ...

c   ... The examples I've provided do not, I think, *obviously*
     belong in the categories to which I've assigned them. That's
     not to say they are weak or wrong but to observe that when
     it comes to any kind of 'gut feeling', it is almost impossible
     to say what is driving it.

My hunch about the rain could, for instance, be down to memory or sense perception – the look of the clouds, the 'feel' of the air;
it could equally be a kind of *prayer*. Similarly, my love for my father
may be ingrained instinct, but it could be the result of 'instruction'.
It might also be said that *love* is so rich, deep and complex a phenomenon that trying to 'explain' it in any way is both unnecessary
and futile. And the intuition that murder is wicked could, equally,
be an *instructed* notion that owes more to teaching than to feeling.[22]
It may occur to you that I've chosen a highly frustrating way
in which to conclude a survey of why we think as we do. That
triple-entry is not only indeterminate in itself, but seems to undermine the validity, or at least the precision, of *all* our reasons.
Well, yes and no – but chiefly 'no', in that numbers 10–12 confirm
three vital things:

• How *similar* are many of our reasons, even though their range
  as an entire collection is formidable.
• In many instances we may have *more than one reason* for
  stating, believing or doing something.[23]
• A host of things which I/we may claim to know are not appre-
  hended *cerebrally*. That emphatically does not make those
  things worthless; on the contrary, it suggests – irresistibly – that
  there is more to human wisdom and the life of the brain than
  can be attributed to the 'mere' power of reasoning. And among
  all else, that neatly sets up the final section of this chapter.

Justifying your thinking II: good instincts

Sense perception

So far I have kept references to specific philosophers to a minimum.
That is because I know that while some readers might share my

delighted interest in the whole subject, the majority probably do not; furthermore, there is more to philosophy than all individual philosophers put together. You can become an extremely able practical thinker without having read a word of Aristotle, Descartes, Kant, Nietzsche, whoever: that indeed has been my aim throughout these explorations. But we have now arrived at a topic which is best introduced by considering a theory put forward by an eighteenth-century philosopher, Bishop George Berkeley.

It is a truism that our senses sometimes deceive us. Many works of philosophy and/or psychology devote a lot of attention and space to optical illusions; I have to say that I've never quite understood why. Yes, they're instructive and entertaining – for about twenty minutes or so; then I begin to ask, 'Well, so what?'. That may be impatient or just foolish – but not half so foolish as those that argue that because our senses occasionally delude us, it is wise to assume that they *always* do.

Berkeley took the latter proposition to its logical (or loony) extreme. He argued that all our senses, all our experience and very awareness of life were *imaginary*, or at any rate could not be proved to be otherwise. That left him open to accusations of declaring the world and all it contains to be meaningless – a tricky spot for any philosopher to be in, but incalculably more so for one who was also a senior servant of God. He got out of jail (maybe literally) by coining the notorious proposition, *esse est percipi*: 'to be is to be perceived'. In Berkeley's paradigm the perceiver is God: he sees all of us at all times and in all places, and therefore we exist after all. So that's all right then, isn't it?

It is almost incredible that anybody took this idea seriously even in Berkeley's time, when the faculty of reason was regarded as proof of man's intrinsic and noble superiority over all other species. Nowadays we are a lot less sure that *Homo sapiens* constitutes Nature's last and best word; yet there are still many highly intelligent men and women who rate Berkeley's ideas as something other than five-star rubbish. Why?

Well, history abounds with instances that suggest you can persuade someone to believe *anything* provided s/he is clever enough; convincing the less clever is often more difficult, or indeed impossible. And that is why I've included this section in a book catering for high-flying students. You might think that there is enough to engage your mind without worrying about whether you live in a state of constant and absolute illusion, and I'd say you'd be right. Yet ideas will always interest the intelligent, and because we live so much through our senses, the notion that they are dangerously fallible can seduce you into backwaters when you need to be in midstream.

Scepticism is an invaluable tool for any student, and that applies here too. By all means be aware that your senses will deceive you at times; so will your intellect, instincts, feelings and every other aspect of your make-up. But those things are all you've got, and not to trust any of them on principle is a very short cut to madness.[24]

There is another reason for having undertaken that baleful survey. The notion that sense perception is intrinsically suspect tends to fuel the related suspicion of something the ambitious student needs to cultivate rather than fear.

The importance of first impressions

Don't judge a book by its cover.

That injunction masquerading as wisdom is dangerous nonsense.

Like most bad proverbs, it doesn't even work on a literal level.[25] The entire publishing industry, then and now, devotes enormous attention and expense to making their products eye-catching – and that primarily means designing a cover that will appeal and stimulate. Moreover, and notwithstanding that last point, even the most cerebrally challenged punters are unlikely to assess a book's quality on the basis of its up-front artwork.

It is on the metaphorical level, though, where the real problems lie. First, if you extend the concept of 'cover' from *books* to *faces*, the proverb is fundamentally at odds with human behaviour and response. Nine times out of ten (at least) we form an opinion of someone by considering the face. Sometimes, yes, we'll be mistaken but – back to those bogus sense perception quandaries – that does not mean we will *always* or even *usually* be wrong. I think Edwin M. Stanton was correct in observing

A man of fifty is responsible for his face

and the great P.G. Wodehouse extended that principle to younger souls:

Gilt The child (drank) Cyril in for about half a minute; then he gave his verdict:

'Fish-face!'

'Eh? What?' said Cyril.

The child, who had evidently been taught at his mother's knee to speak the truth, made his meaning a trifle clearer.

'You've a face like a fish!'

He spoke as if Cyril was more to be pitied than censured, which I'm bound to say I thought rather decent and broad-minded of him. I don't mind admitting that, whenever I looked at Cyril's face, I always had a feeling that he couldn't have got that way without it being mostly his own fault.[26]

If to say that we get the face we deserve borders on harshness, it is nonetheless true that our physiognomy says a great deal about us, especially to others.

Second – and where this proverbial drivel becomes toxic rather than merely idiotic or contentious – in declaring that outward appearances are inherently misleading, it encourages the further idea that *all* immediate responses are invariably wrong. No they are not. On the contrary, 80 per cent of the time (an approximate figure, but I'll stick to it) *first impressions are right*. Remember that each time you encounter a new literary text, maths problem, geographical map, historical document, scientific theory, so on and so forth; especially remember it when reading an examination question for the first time.

Naturally, you must *reconsider and test* those first impressions. To assume that they are automatically right is as foolish as the assumption that they are always mistaken. But what we notice first has great impact, and our instincts are in the main as reliable as our more sober, leisurely judgements. The best policy here is a 'both/and' one: look to harmonise your antennae and your thinking brain. The combination will serve you well, not least because, more often than not, you will find that your instant thoughts are both confirmed and deepened by your subsequent reasoning. As Oscar Wilde put it:

It is only shallow people who do not judge by appearances.

That witty paradox is an enabling truth; you could do worse than make it a guiding motto. In any event, go on judging books by their covers for as long as it illuminates and energises – and it will.

Our very last port of call is a return visit.

The value of the hunch

The hunch might qualify as just a particular kind of 'first impression' were it not that it often makes itself felt *before* one's initial look at something or somebody. Earlier I defined it as 'a gut feeling'; an analogous but brain-related term might be 'advance subconscious intelligence'. Both point to an intuition that arrives out of the blue before the forebrain has started its work.

Since it pre-dates any empirical or forensic evidence, it is tempting to see a hunch as the antithesis of 'scientific method'. Yet the history of science abounds in instances of discoveries that began in instinctive belief. Here's an example furnished by Professor C.A. Mace.

> **When Torricelli inverted a tube of mercury, thereby inventing the barometer, and when Florin Perier carried his barometer up the Puy de Dome to observe the influence of altitude, they did not do these things merely to 'see what would happen.' They must have had *a shrewd idea in advance.* Otherwise their conduct would have been eccentric.**[27]   [My italics]

The italicised phrase provides another definition of a hunch – a splendid one which can also be applied to the now-legendary work of Francis Crick and James Watson. When they started their laboratory investigations into the structure of DNA, both were already convinced its shape was a double-helix; all they needed to do was to prove it! It took them years, but they succeeded – and much later Crick had this to say about their procedures:

> **It is true that in blundering about, we found gold, but the fact remains we were looking for gold – asking the right question.**[28]

'A shrewd idea in advance'; 'asking the right question'. Both should be part of your armoury as you strive for those straight 'A's.

Conclusion

Most of this chapter has been driven by 'Epistemology'. That sumptuous word denotes:

The branch of philosophy that concerns itself with the varieties, grounds and validity of knowledge.

As you will have gathered once or twice, for all my absorbed interest in matters epistemological, there have been – and will continue to be – more than a few occasions when they strike me as the biggest waste of time and talent you'll find outside an advertising agency.[29] Nevertheless, *thinking about thinking* is not only interesting fun, at least most of the time. It is an activity which can only increase one's ability to distinguish what is important from what is trivial; what is worthwhile from what is worthless; perhaps above all, what is sound from what is suspect. And any bright hungry student needs that awareness in full.

Chapter 5

Doing it

Preliminary

The three activities on which this chapter focuses

- reading
- note-taking
- writing essays and assignments

are central to all study, and most Study Skills Guides devote considerable time and space to them. However, much of the resultant material is elementary and foundational, and while that observation does not imply even the slightest sneer at the provision of such advice, I am going to assume that you do not need it. Any student realistically aiming for a clutch of top grades is almost certain to be soundly versed in all three areas.

Moreover, it is my recent experience (both in my own institution and outside it) that today's students are more proficient in note-taking than was the case a decade ago; to a large extent that also applies to planning and writing assignments and to coping with their reading-loads. And touching on this book's layout and concerns thus far: if (as I hope) you found the previous chapter not only clear but invigorating, it is most unlikely that you now require any lengthy advice about how to absorb academic material productively, the need to avoid the kind of vacuous introductions that characterise pedestrian essays, or the use of 'spidergrams'.[1]

So my intention is to go beyond the 'ordinary', offering instead a selection of 'advanced tips' designed to extend your control as you progress and increase your mastery when you come to perform.

Eyes right: speed-reading

I begin by cannibalising something I wrote many years ago:

> **You pick up the book, find the chapter at issue and start reading. All may be well for a while; but by the time you're into the second page, things are getting rather foggy. You struggle on, reach the end of the page – and then, suddenly, you realise about halfway down your third page that you've hardly taken in a thing. Not only have you lost your way: you can't even remember what territory you're in or what the map suggested.**

That happens to us all at one time or another, but such universality doesn't make the experience any less undesirable. To realise that you've just thrown away five-plus minutes of study-time when at your freshest is bad enough, but there are worse things than mere waste. Your confidence, enjoyment and success will be seriously threatened by these further consequences:

• You will feel stupidly inefficient.
• You will have to read the material again. That is likely to feel like a punishment for 'bad work'.
• As a result, you will probably undertake that revisit in a mood of sour resentment . . .
• . . . And it's therefore likely that your second attempt will be only marginally more productive, reactivating the whole sorry experience and deepening both your depression and the hole that you're now in.
• In all, this amounts to *snail-reading* of the worst kind.

Bad news indeed. Fortunately, the good news is that the experience is easily avoided and a strategy readily available to ensure reading that is sensibly fast, efficient and enjoyable. All you need do is remind yourself every time you embark upon academic reading that:

• The material will have to be read at least twice and probably more before you can confidently assume mastery.

That may seem an uncomfortable, even forbidding truth, but it has two hugely liberating corollaries:

1   How you go about such plural reading is entirely your affair
    . . .

2   . . . Which means that you can make your first reading an
    exercise in reconnaissance rather than attempted absorption.

The latter is very close to what we do when browsing in a
bookshop or a library, and although the student's concerns are
much more rigorous than the casual browser's, the policy is still
admirably effective. A quick though alert skim-read will enable
you to trace the outline of the material's territory and a number
of its main features. To achieve that kind of overall map will not
take you long (say, ten minutes for a twenty-page chapter), and
it will empower both your intellectual focus and your confidence.

You may then opt for a fiercely focused second reading which
looks to give you control of the material, or you may wish to do
it in further stages. As noted, it does not matter how you do it:
the end result – full and satisfying absorption – is all that counts.
However, there is one thing to be said for perusing such text
several times: once you reach the third reading:

**You will be engaged upon a *critical dialogue* with the
author**

whereby you will have gone beyond dutiful absorption and be
appraising the material in true academic fashion. That does not
necessarily mean that you will be finding fault with it or anything
comparably negative; it simply involves you in a 'meeting of
minds' which can only strengthen your grasp and therefore your
ambitions.

I could go on to describe a number of speed-reading programmes,
but I'm not going to. As ambitious students, you will I'm sure be
convinced of the need to read as time-efficiently as possible. As
bright students you will almost certainly be able to devise a system
of your own. If you do require some help in this direction, the
Bibliography will point you in several productive directions; however, as with mnemonics, the best system is one you *create* rather
than follow. All I'll add before moving on is this further brief piece
of cannibalisation:

**Serious reading of any kind is a gradual process, in
the sense that full understanding can never be**

immediate. Anything worthwhile requires several readings before it can be mastered. The decision to make most of them as rapid and pleasant as possible is not a dishonest shortcut but a properly intelligent way of bringing that moment forward.[2]

So far, my advice has presupposed the reading of 'printed material' – books, articles, pamphlets and so on. These days, however, a good deal of student reading is of a quite different kind which requires a section to itself.

Eyes wrong: screen-reading

In Chapter 3 we looked at white space – that textual feature that makes your readers well-disposed towards you because you've taken the trouble to make their task as comfortable as you can. Such 'public' duty is as admirable as it is wise; no less important, however, is the provision of white space when you are engaged on 'private' duties as a reader yourself.

Screen-reading is now integral to our daily life and work, and the practice is going to grow, not diminish. Whoever we are and whatever our job, concerns or ambit, we are all going to spend an increasing amount of our time glued to a PC screen. That's the new way of the world, and there is nothing to be done about it. Nor do I want to suggest that this controlling circumstance is a bad thing: as I've observed more than once already, the enabling properties of the PC should be properly celebrated and properly exploited. But to my mind:

Screen-reading is a fundamentally unnatural activity.

You may not agree. It is likely that computers were as much a part of your childhood as toys and books, whereas I had turned forty before I bought my first word processor, let alone a PC. That means I had to learn and acclimatise myself to a number of things which for you had become everyday skills by the time you were ten or even younger, and it might occur to you that I'm just an ageing Prisoner of History. Possibly; but chatting to my own students just before I wrote these pages, more than a few declared a similar aversion to screen-reading, citing these important drawbacks:

1   After twenty minutes my eyes seem to have dried out and focusing is really difficult.

2   You can't add marginal notes even to your own stuff, and much downloaded text is 'read only', protected.

3   You can't hold a screen.

4   The screen seems to control me in a way that doesn't happen when I read books or printed material.

5   After a while – particularly if it's my own work – I don't see what is actually written but what I 'know' to be there.

6   No matter what the font or spacing, the text is unrestful, if not downright intimidating.

Points 4 and 6 crucially return us to white space. As I type these words, there is a fair chunk of it to the right, but none to the left. The numbered items just above are somewhat broken up, yes, but in a short while those breaks will disappear off the top of the screen, giving my eyes no respite from my own amorphous text. As a result, not only am I certain to make mistakes:

I probably won't notice *half* of them until I see that work in hard-copy form.

That introduces *the* most important tip I can offer, whether you're researching or composing, for it embraces all six problems just listed and a number of other potential ones too.

As soon as you can or it is sensible, print out what you've been scanning and read it in your own space and time.

If possible, remove yourself from your PC area while doing so, or at least firmly turn your face away from it. As a result, no longer dictated to by a white-space free zone, you will once again be in charge, able to handle and annotate the material (points 2 and 3 above) and also check what is written as opposed to assumed (point 5).

The ill-effects which excessive screen-reading can cause to a student are comparable to the condition known as 'Repetitive Strain Injury' suffered by office workers. Like the similarly debilitating 'ME',[3] 'RSI' has few obvious symptoms and there is nothing organically wrong with those affected by it it. They may not even feel remotely ill in any 'normal' way: they are just enormously frustrated in being unable to do their work in the way they want to do it, when they want to do it and with the equipment provided for them to do it.[4]

What I will call 'Screen-Reading Syndrome' (SRS) won't affect the student's operational competence in quite the same way, but the damage it can do is just as significant. This is because it is both insidious and unseen: no-one can diagnose it except the reader. Those six observations voiced by my students are striking and eloquent, but they wouldn't impress a doctor – or to put it another, probably more accurate way, there's nothing a doctor could do about it. Except to say what I've said:

> **Don't do it. Or if you *must* do it – and I admit that a certain amount of screen-reading is nowadays unavoidable – keep it under strict control.**

SRS might be regarded as a swanky variant of that old favourite 'eye-strain'. That would be unfair, chiefly because it's quite untrue, as this paradox[5] looks to demonstrate:

> **You don't read with the eye, you read with the *brain*.**

If that were not so, nobody could solve anagrams or indeed any cryptic-crossword clue; translate from a foreign language; decode contracts, government forms and legal documents; or read a newspaper headline upside-down (a daily occurrence in millions of trains all over the world). Nor would it be possible for you to decode this next passage as easily as I suspect you will:

> **A**
> **Aoccdrnig to a rscheheacr at Cmabrigde Uinervtisy, it deosn't mttaer in waht oredr the ltteers in a wrod are, the olny iprmoetnt tihng is taht the frist and lsat ltteer be at the rghit pclae. The rset can be a toatl mses and you can sitll raed it wouthit porbelm. Tihs is bcuseae the huamn mnid deos not raed ervey lteter by istlef, but the wrod as a wlohe.**

That text circulated on the Internet in September 2003, and it has since become the basis of significant research in psycho-linguistics.

That may or may not interest you, but I hope you *were* intrigued by how quickly you could make sense of what at first sight seems mumbo-jumbo. Just for the record, the 'true' version reads:

B

According to a researcher at Cambridge University, it doesn't matter in what order the letters in a word are, the only important thing is that the first and last letter be at the right place. The rest can be a total mess and you can still read it without problem. This is because the human mind does not read every letter by itself but the word as a whole.

For all that you may be pleased to have solved that riddle, you wouldn't want to read such 'A' material very often or for very long, and that's because what is at issue is not eye-strain but 'brain-strain'. Truly efficient reading depends on giving the material your full attention, which becomes rapidly more difficult to do when staring at an uncompromising and 'unholdable' screen; increasingly it becomes a dour slog, whereas decoding six jumbled lines is at least challenging *fun*.

My last point revisits and extends the observations about email made in Chapter 3. There I was concerned with alerting you to dangers of haste and the often-consequent ignoring of mechanical accuracy or even sense. Here I'd like to make these further observations:

1   All emails that I've ever received or seen in hard copy are 10-font jobs that are distinctly unpleasant to read . . .
2   . . . They are additionally cramped and error-ridden.
3   On the screen, they have no white space. When/if you print them out, there's *masses* of it – but all in the wrong places (as in the frozen wastes of blank paper following the message).
4   Number 3 applies even more when you 'reply to sender': you have no 'eye-room' at all.
5   The great majority of emails are written 'on-line' and then sent without print-out checking. That's why they are often not sufficiently clear as well as being error-ridden. So . . .
6   . . . If an email is truly important to you, compose it first as a Word document; print it out; check it; then – and *only* then – send it.

Here and there, my observations about SRS may strike you as fanciful. I don't think they are: I am convinced that you will prosper best as a high-flying student if you stick, largely, to the reading of the printed word that has served humanity pretty well since Caxton's invention of the printing-press in the late fifteenth century. Quite apart from anything else, that kind of reading is simply more *enjoyable*, both physically and mentally, than staring at a screen – and by now I hope I don't need to emphasise how important is pleasure to anyone who wants to do well.

Now on to an activity that is intimately related to academic reading and indeed interlocks with it.

Note-taking

> I have noted it well.
> *King Lear*, Act I, Scene iv

If my experience is at all representative, students today are far more clued-up about good note-taking than were their counterparts twenty or even ten years ago. So, in keeping with my avoidance of all 'cat-sat-on-the-mat' advice, I am going to assume that you are:

• Aware that your notes are your *private* business. Not only are they not going to be marked or appraised: provided you are clear about what they signify, they don't even have to make sense to anybody else.

• Familiar with Keyword Noting and other such 'gutting' techniques.

• Comfortable with whatever methods you employ – be they the use of highlighters, different colours, underlining, marginal commentary, shorthand codes, whatever – and serene about sticking with them as long as they go on working for you.

• Alert to the dangers of taking *too many notes* during a class or a lecture – you can't write and listen properly at the same time.

• Attuned to taking notes at *different stages* of your learning process, and to adapting their form according to each specific purpose and need.

As a result, you can confidently identify with King Lear's remark above.

However, I suspect there is one area where some advice might be profitable, and I will introduce it by quoting an opinion voiced by a colleague whose wisdom I normally value very much.

Rewriting class notes is a waste of time.

I could not agree less.

Naturally, *mere duplicatory copying* is pointless. But his remark has unfortunate implications: it encourages students to think that *any* revisiting of their notes is comparably futile.

That is quite untrue: to *update, clarify* and *add to* your notes is a very valuable and important thing to do.

Virtually all students are aware that notes taken during the earliest weeks of their course are fundamental to their under-standing and progress, and high-flyers invariably make that 'base' a high priority. All well and good; however, that term 'progress' needs to be dwelt on a little further.

The timescale for those embarking on a new programme of study is astonishingly compressed. A British Prime Minister (Harold Wilson, 1967) once remarked that 'A week is a long time in politics,' but that's nothing compared to the time-warp experi-enced by most students – be they aged fourteen, sixteen, eighteen or beyond – in the first two months of their course. By week eight, say, even moderate students will be noticeably more knowledge-able about their subjects than they were in weeks one and two, and high-flyers are likely to be prodigiously so. In view of that, does it not make sense to reconsider those notes taken six weeks ago, bringing them into line with what you now know and indeed *are*? Isn't that what progress means and involves?

The fact remains that a great many students do *not* practise such 'revisionist noting', and you may be one of them. Don't go on making that mistake. The undertaking won't take you long,[6] and it brings these immediate and major benefits:

- It will, beyond doubt, improve your grasp of the material at issue.
- It will allow you to 'up-grade' good fundamental insights into something more fleshed-out and therefore more enabling.

- It will noticeably boost your confidence, for three reasons:

  a   You will be pleasingly aware that you're taking good care of business.
  b   You will almost immediately see how far you've travelled since those first weeks.
  c   You will be able almost to *feel* your mind expanding and your knowledge growing. At the start of the course your brain's storage capacity might have resembled a VHS tape; now it has DVD dimensions!

- Best of all (I would argue), such critical perusal may well inspire fresh ideas that would not otherwise have come to you.
- Finally, such in-built revisionist rhythms will make your final revision for exams both easier and more productive – a bonus we shall reaffirm in Chapter 6.

Mini Lecture Noting Exercise

That is all the 'advanced advice' on note-taking I am assuming you need. But before we move onto the crunch-issue of the writing of essays, reports and all formal assignments, let me test that assumption – and you – via an exercise. I want you to 'note' the 800-word passage which follows on pp. 115–16. Its first few paragraphs should be familiar – I used them to demonstrate the virtues of white space in Chapter 3 – and I hope that makes the task a little more comfortable.

The piece was originally composed as a short lecture. It is not in any real sense 'difficult', but though I say it myself, it contains very little obvious *flab*. That means that you'll have some fairly subtle decisions to make about what is crucial as opposed to merely interesting.

Procedure and advice

- How you go about this is your own affair. You may wish to read it silently, annotating and highlighting as you go, and then look over it again to check that you've got all that you think really matters.
- However, you may prefer to have it read *to* you by a friend or member of the family. If taking the latter option, it may

ELVIS PRESLEY'S SYMBOLIC DECLINE

The story of Elvis Presley is one that is not only both tragic and tacky but also decisively, almost symbolically, American.

When he burst on the scene in the mid-1950s, Presley was a talent as shocking for some as he was exciting for others, full of a raw power whose sexuality was almost tangible. (Within months, any below-waist shots of Elvis performing were banned on US TV and newsreel.) He drew on the separate-yet-linked traditions of hillbilly music and the blues, a potent combination made all the more exciting by a voice at once true and husky and a rhythmic flair that no other mass-selling artist has ever approached. And to quote one of his 1958 hits, Elvis was 'Trouble'. In an America gripped by the Cold-War-dominated ethos of the Eisenhower years and for whom McCarthyism was still an issue, the youthful rebellion and sheer energy that Presley embodied were not only alarming but indecent to the point of un-Americanness. Marxism was, in Robert Hughes's phrase, 'America's nurturing enemy', and anything or anyone who diverted the nation's zeal from focusing on the 'Red Menace' was bad news – 'trouble' in abundance.

Some of you may have an idea of what happened next. Presley remained a 'dangerous', youth-oriented singer for another two or so years, during which time he had an unbroken string of hits that mined further the earthiness of his first records, e.g. *Jailhouse Rock*, *I Got Stung*, *Big Hunk Of Love* and *Hard-Headed Woman*. Even while America's young was rocking and rolling to such joyous and seemingly anarchic sounds, though, a softening-up process was going on. Colonel Tom Parker, Presley's manager, had already determined that Elvis would become an all-round family entertainer, for reasons that had as much to do with small-town conservative values as with money. (For Parker, the two things were intimately related, if not synonymous.) In 1958 Presley went into the army. Unsurprisingly (it must now be said) he emerged as the model soldier, all modest dutifulness and artful (that is to say *coached*) gung-ho patriotism. By the time he was demobbed, middle – and *middle-aged* – America had already taken him to their hearts, and Parker's long-term plan streamrollered into action.

For a while there were still glimpses of the 'old' Elvis – songs like *Stuck On You, Such A Night, Feel So Bad, Good Luck Charm*, and the 1963 *Devil In Disguise*, which in the view of many was his very last rock record of true quality. But these were mixed up with and into a schmaltz of increasing remorselessness – *Are You Lonesome Tonight?*, the cringingly devout *Crying In The Chapel* and, an all too significant title, *Sentimental Me*. At the same time his conveyor-belt movies accelerated in both frequency and lousiness. Initially Elvis had been a striking actor (very powerful in *King Creole*, based on Harold Robbins's *A Stone For Danny Fisher*, and also impressive in *Jailhouse Rock* and *Flaming Star*), but now his every cinematic outing was an exercise in semi-idiocy, occasionally alleviated by the odd good song.

Grimly eloquent is this information unearthed in 2002 by Glyn Brown: 'Shockingly, we discover that Presley was offered parts in *Midnight Cowboy*, *West Side Story*, the Kris Kristofferson role in *A Star Is Born* – which he begged to do but the percentage wasn't high enough for the Colonel. Instead, we had Elvis in *Fun In Acapulco* (playing a sea-going trapeze artist), in *Harum Scarum*, in *Girls, Girls, Girls.*' Brown gleaned this from *Elvis: By Those Who Knew Him Best* by Rose Clayton and Dick Heard (Virgin), one of two new books on Presley reviewed in Brown's article for *The Times* in July 2002.[7]

Many commentators argue that Presley enjoyed a revival in the 1970s. That may have been true commercially, but it is hard to see his recordings of that time as anything but a pale, crowd-pleasing shadow of his earlier work. That astonishing voice remained more or less unimpaired to the end, but his rhythmic sense became almost as sluggish as his increasingly bloated physique, and he was no more exciting than other middle-aged survivors such as Tom Jones and Englebert Humperdink. Unlike them, though, Presley did not survive for very long. His increasingly destructive, even insane lifestyle took its ultimate toll in the summer of 1977, when Elvis died. He was forty-two.

Nor is it easy to understand why his appeal and iconic status remain undimmed nearly thirty years on. The still-electric quality of his early records may partly explain it; yet the 'Elvis Lives!' clan – and it's a very big clan – celebrate *everything* he recorded with the same uncritical devotion. Perhaps one answer lies in Presley's definitive American-ness. A once-thrilling, wondrously energetic and original talent all too rapidly descended into sentimentality, sterile economics and, ultimately, sanctimonious self-destruction. The story of Elvis furnishes a disturbing model of America itself.

help you to know that I estimate its duration to be seven minutes when delivered at a speed less deliberate than dictation but (obviously) gentler than normal speech.

- Your governing task is to attempt to identify

  1   utterly fundamental material
  2   primary/essential material
  3   secondary material
  4   merely illustrative or ultimately marginal material

  and tailor your note-taking accordingly.

- If you do this as well as I'm expecting you to, you can safely consider yourself a highly accomplished note-taker whose skills are assured and permanent. You may even produce a better version than the 'answer' you'll find in Appendix II.

Writing

> Most thinkers write badly, because they communicate not only their thoughts, but the thinking of them.
>
> Nietzsche

All the skills and techniques explored in this book are important to students, but 'writing' arguably matters most of all, if only because your assignments and therefore your final grades depend on it. That is one reason why it forms the climax to this chapter, but there's a different kind of logic that also informs my decision to leave it till last. 'Reading' is, it goes without saying, the most fundamental study-activity, from the first browsing perusal to the acquisition of real authority. 'Note-taking', especially of the advanced kind we've been concerned with here, is a mixture of contemplation and composition – or to put it more simply, of reading and writing.

I make that rather obvious point because it is my experience that good note-takers – which I take you to be after your 'Elvis Presley' success – are good writers too. I don't think it's possible to take truly productive notes without having a highly developed grasp not only of the material being read but also of how the writing *works*, what makes it good (or bad) and why certain things matter more to you than others. And that invariably seems to result in such awareness and control characterising your own writing too.

That is not to suggest that I imagine you're a perfect writer (any more than I am), but it does mean that we need waste no time on rudimentary matters. I assume your spelling, grammar, sentence-structure to be in good order; I'm even more confident that your punctuation and paragraphing are likewise, given the attention paid to those techniques in Chapter 3. I also assume that you know the dangers of pleasant introductions which say absolutely nothing or of rambling on for the sake of space-filling (it fools nobody and irritates everyone), and how decisively impressive a conclusion both crisp and short can be. Instead, here are some further advanced tips which will make your good writing even better – sharper and more appealing.

Those tips centre on four properties fundamental to any and all successful writing:

1   knowing precisely what you have – or want – to do;
2   good tempo;
3   genuine analysis, not mere description;
4   a proper sense of *you*.

Do what you're told and what you say

Whatever it is you're writing – a report, an essay, an exam answer – it will have a title. If it's one of your own devising, make sure you actually address – *in full* – what it telegraphs; the same goes for any question you've been set.

You might think that to offer high-flying students such elementary advice is snootily unnecessary. I'm afraid it isn't. As the story in Chapter 1 hinging on the difference between 'describe' and 'explain' partly illustrates (see pp. 17–19), able candidates underachieve far more often by misreading questions than by being underprepared or inadequately taught. Sometimes, too, it's not so much a careless lack of alertness as to what the question requires as simple linguistic ignorance: I am surprised by how many good students have a less than precise grasp of the difference between 'analyse', 'criticise', 'evaluate', 'identify' and so on. If you are one such student, please look closely at the following table. I hope certain things become clearer as a result; however, I suspect you will need to re-read it at some stage, and I especially recommend you do so the night before any exam.

COMMAND VERBS

— **Account for**	Explain the cause of
— **Analyse**	Separate down into component parts and show how they interrelate with each other
— **Comment on**	Make critical or explanatory notes/observations
— **Compare**	Point out the differences and similarities
— **Contrast**	Point out differences only and present result in orderly fashion
— **Criticise**	Make judgements through reasoned discussion and consistently supported by evidence
— **Describe**	Write down the information in the right order
— **Differentiate**	Look for differences between[8]
— **Discuss**	Present arguments for and against the topic in question; you can also give your opinion
— **Distinguish**	See **Differentiate**
— **Enumerate**	List or specify
— **Evaluate**	Estimate the value of, looking at positive and negative attributes
— **Explain**	Give reasons; say 'why' rather than just define
— **Identify**	Select features according to the question
— **Justify**	Show adequate grounds for decisions or conclusions
— **List**	Item by item consideration of the topic, usually presented one under the other
— **Outline**	Give the main features or general features of a subject, omitting minor details and stressing structure
— **Prove**	Demonstrate truth/falsehood via evidence
— **Relate**	1 Narrate 2 Show connection between events/facts
— **Review**	Make a survey of the subject, examining it critically
— **Summarise**	State the main features of an argument, omitting all that is only partially relevant
— **Trace**	Follow the development of the topic/issue

Aim for pace and variety

The introductory term 'good tempo' used in the list above is inspired by chess rather than music, and indicates the ability to render every move vigorous and meaningful. Desirable in itself, it carries the major bonus of strengthening position and sharpening attack.

Exactly the same is true of all good prose.

Good writing has no flab, no sentences which mark time, nothing that isn't crisply considered, and certainly nothing that qualifies as mere 'thinking aloud'. The quotation from Nietzsche which heads this section is as enabling as it is stern: if you avoid cluttering up your essay with the mechanics of thinking and instead deliver only the finished thought, the results will invariably please and impress.

That is not easy to accomplish, because you have to be constantly on your guard – especially at the beginning of a written task.[9] At the start of this chapter I dismissed any chance of you perpetrating long-windedly empty opening paragraphs, but you may be prone to subtler flaws. Here are two otherwise excellent introductions (written by seventeen-year-olds in the second term of their IBO course) slightly tarnished by the title-paraphrase. Note that in each case the fault does not occur at the *start* of the first paragraph but at the *end*:

> A Title: Which comes out worse, 'Civilisation' or 'The Primitive' in Joseph Conrad's *Heart of Darkness*?
>
> The novel explores the differences between the 'civilised' (the Europeans) and the 'primitive' (the natives of Africa). Marlow the narrator focuses more or less equally on both, and we recognise his view of white and civilised superiority over the primitive African. But he also demonstrates his recognition, more subtle but no less telling, that the European colonisers – and he himself – are not as superior as they imagine. Some might say that the 'primitives' *must* come out worse, as they have less structure to their society, still carry out ritualistic traditions and do things which 'civilised' countries would view as 'uncivilised'. *But in this essay I will look at both the 'civilised' and the 'primitive' and see whether the colonisers do come out on top.* [My italics]

B Title: Given that *Heart of Darkness* is almost unrelievedly a tale of doom, gloom and entropy, why does it fascinate and exhilarate so?

Heart of Darkness is an imprecise plunge into human nature, an exploring examination of the potential darkness within us all which can be released given the right circumstances. I realise that opening sounds just as vague as much of Conrad's script, but while I hope it is not too much of a paradox, I believe that vagueness to be immensely important to defining Conrad's meaning. Just as Kurtz and Marlow both had individual experiences in the Congo which morphed them from the wholesome men they were into the drained beings they become, each reader must individually experience the text and build their own mental picture of what the words mean. *This essay will explain my interpretation of the work.* [My italics]

Those were and remain notable efforts from students in the early stages of a demanding course, and they preface what went on to become accounts of considerable distinction. Yet the italicised sentences are surely useless, saying nothing that is not implicit in the titles chosen or already impressively explicit in the sentences which precede them.

You could argue that each was a momentary aberration, even the tiniest slip, and in these instances I would not quarrel overmuch. But a lot of students seem to feel duty-bound to include remarks like this, and I do not recommend it. I know that in some institutions students are encouraged to:

Say what you're going to say and then say it – and when you've said it, say you've said it. (SWYGTSATSI – AWYSISYSI)

This may be sensible advice to the very moderate or struggling performer who otherwise has little hope of structuring a coherent argument, but for students as good as the two quoted above it is not only quite unnecessary but subtly destructive. It takes just four or five outbreaks of SWYGTSATSI–AWYSISYSI or something comparably vacuous to sacrifice tempo – not ruinously, maybe, but enough to make a difference.

Tempo is also assisted by 'variety' – by which I mean varying your sentence length and, occasionally, even the size of your paragraphs.[10] Too many long, complex sentences dull your impact and become laborious to read even if the material is of high quality. On the other hand, a succession of short, one-clause sentences soon acquires a stuttery feel, damaging fluency and disrupting the reader's concentration. Look to mix them up. There's no need to be obsessive about this, deploying your sentences on a 'two long, one short, one long, two short ...' basis like some ludicrous prose equivalent of Morse Code. All that's required is one – or preferably both – of these two checking mechanisms:

1   *Listen* to what you write as you go.
2   Periodically look over what you've already written.

The first is not an easy habit to acquire, but it's well worth the effort. The writer's ear is a very good friend, communicating a sense of pace, rhythm and clarity: if any of those are deficient, you'll 'hear' it before you see it. Acting on that not only enables you to put it right faster but soon establishes a governing aural awareness of your work which means there will be less and less to put right in the first place. It is no accident that all good conversation or discussion reads well when transcribed, and the converse is equally true: good prose has an immediate intimacy and a strong sense of *voice*.

The second is an excellent idea anyway, especially when writing exam answers – which is why I shall return to it in the final chapter. But if variety is your immediate goal, such re-perusal will alert you to anything amiss. Over-long sentences can quickly be adjusted, as can a succession of short ones via the use of semi-colons or colons instead of full stops; in addition, you will be more sharply on guard when you resume writing.

A pleasing feature in its own right, variety also assists 'pace'; together they should ensure that your prose is attractively *supple*. That desirable aim also informs this next section.

Muscle, not flab: analysis 'versus' description

Needless to say, 'description' has its place in academic work. If that were not so, 'describe' would not be one of the twenty-one command verbs tabled in the previous section. Moreover, a number of assignments in several subjects – among them the sciences, geography, art – require you first to describe what you

saw or what you did, and you must of course obey such proce-
dural instructions. But the operative word in that previous
sentence is first. If *all* you do is describe, no matter what the
subject or the task, you aren't going to get very far, and you
certainly aren't going to get that top grade.

All that said and decidedly meant, I am aware that many good
students take quite a while to become aware of the practical (i.e.
mark-scoring) difference between description and analysis. So let's
briefly revisit those command verbs definitions:

1 *Describe*   Write down the information in the right order.
2 *Analyse*   Separate down into component parts and show
                how they interrelate with each other.

As noted, you may be required to accomplish no. 1 during the
early stages of certain tasks – and if you are asked to 'summarise'
or 'précis' material, you must ruthlessly bypass your own
opinions and reactions, functioning as an 'intelligent scribe' only.
But in most other instances, sooner rather than later you will
need to operate as something more vigorous. You will need to
make the material *yours* – by demonstrating how you think it
works, what connections you notice, how the different aspects of
what you're dealing with affect each other, and (in the case
of Humanities subjects certainly) how it affects *you*. It doesn't
make much difference whether what you *separate down into
component parts* is a poem, a chemical compound or a car engine:
you are in charge of it, actively exploring rather than passively
recording.

Mere description is particularly destructive in literary answers,
for there it takes the form of 'telling the story'. It is astonishing
how many able students do this until they are cajoled or bullied
out of it! In such tasks you can – indeed *must* – assume that your
marker has read the text in question and knows it thoroughly,
and that at top-grade level:

Zero credit is awarded to trotting out *what happens*.

The instructional motto I give my own students runs

**Tell me things I *don't* know, i.e. what's in your
head.**

I believe that can help all students, not just those doing literature. Once you are determined to make the material your own preserve, what you say will decisively reveal your unique thinking, not just the things that you and the reader have in common from the start. And that benefit neatly sets up the chapter's last section.

Make constant use of your biggest asset: you

When I became a man, I put away childish things.

St Paul's words may have become, to borrow a phrase from Sellar and Yeatman's *1066 And All That*, 'utterly memorable', but they constitute dangerous advice for anyone interested in writing well.

Bright children are, naturally,[11] limited writers, but their style is invariably appealing, often very funny, and usually clear and sharp. That judgement owes nothing to sentimentality. Children write in such a fresh way because language itself is still fresh to them. They may not know many words, but because of that, the words they *do* know have a huge charm – almost a touch of magic – and the pleasure they get in using them results in a direct, vibrant style that is itself a pleasure to experience. Once we get used to language, however, its charm can fade, and that decline tends to coincide with that stage in our lives when as often as not we feel awkward and hesitant, are acutely aware of others' awareness of us, and determined above all things not to look foolish.

I am, obviously, talking about 'adolescence' – that time when we scornfully 'put away childish things' without quite under-standing why or knowing what to put in their place. Instead we start to create protective layers of personality, or what the German psychologist Wilhelm Reich defined as 'character armour'. One of the most formidable pieces of that armour is our language and how we deploy it. Whereas the child is quite unthinking and natural in giving tongue, the adolescent is cautious, wary, self-conscious; it is no wonder that as adolescents we first learn to use language to *disguise* or *hide* meaning rather than express it. Now, too, we start to come under the influence of *public* modes of language. We develop an awareness, no matter how vague, of the ways in which politicians, broadcasters and other public figures express themselves; we increasingly recognise properties of 'formal' speech and writing; in short, we become accustomed to adult language. But it needs to be remembered that:

A considerable amount of 'adult' or 'formal' language is ugly, dull, obscure or meaningless – sometimes all four at once.

Of course, at any given time there are countless exceptions to that; indeed, one of the great advances we make as adolescents is learning to appreciate[12] sophisticated language and grasp complex ideas. This is both accompanied and enabled by a prodigious spurt in our vocabulary, sense of form and structure, human insight and intellectual stamina. All that is excellent, but because it's happening simultaneously with a host of other, confusing and intimidating things, the overall combination amounts to a highly potent cocktail that can have toxic consequences. However, there is an antidote – or even more cheeringly, there is an ingredient which if added to that cocktail will neutralise all potential toxicity and make any antidote irrelevant. And it is:

Don't put away childish things – or certainly not the natural 'you' that informed all your childhood writing.

As I've implied, the chief reason why so many students have so much trouble forging a clear and efficient style is that their (invariably good) sense of *what* they want to say is muddied by their confusion about *how* they should say it. Faced with an apparent model by adults in the public eye (and quite a lot of adults who aren't), they set about acquiring the 'correct' approach, the 'right' phrases, the 'impressive' expressions which will guarantee stylistic maturity and weight. That can all too easily result in a style that is indeed 'forged' – i.e. dubious, bogus and above all unnatural.

So try to keep things as simple and punchy as you can. That doesn't mean reverting to childlike vocabulary and a succession of short sentences. You can – and should – deploy your massively increased word-power and structuring technique, but in such a way that:

Every sentence says something you want it to.

Many years ago the late John Leese, then editor of the *Evening Standard*, wrote:

Good ideas are invariably simple; and bad writing will kill any good idea.

To those wise words I would add this corollary:

Any good idea that cannot be expressed simply is not a good idea after all.

On now to a few specific tips about how to ensure your natural voice is also dignified and muscular.

Words and phrases to avoid

I would advise zero tolerance and employment of:

incredibly   literally   basically   definitely   pathetic.

Far too many writers use these too often, too loosely or too weakly – often all three. They are fine in informal speech, but they either do no work or are used without a proper understanding of their meaning.

Be very wary of 'taught structures' such as:

It is interesting to note that . . .
In order to do x, we must first consider y . . .
It is worthy of note that . . .
By way of conclusion it can be argued that . . .

Those four are just exemplars of the kind of pretentious padding that can quickly contaminate formal writing. And the overriding point is that such stuff is not only bloated and inert but *artificial*: no young writer would come up with them naturally or instinctively. They are the result of force-feeding by misguided instructors who consider them nourishing fodder, intrinsic to the health of your essay. They are nothing of the sort: they do no work, waste time and also irritate the reader. Give them the widest possible berth.

Register and 'pitch'

Staying natural does not mean sliding into slang, chatty colloquialism or excessive informality. The last thing I want to encourage in you is anything resembling pomposity, but keep your prose dignified. There are other, sharper ways of making the point than using terms like 'over the top', 'control-freak', 'laid-back' and 'no brainer', and all such idioms carry the additional risk of not being understood by readers who have not encountered them. Stick to standard English: there's a rich storehouse from which to choose!

Reference and quotation

Citing experts and using illustrative quotation are excellent habits to get into, but you need to take care over two matters.

1   All such material must be fully acknowledged and formally referenced.

If you don't do this, you risk charges of 'plagiarism' (whose lethal dangers I covered in Chapter 1) and you will certainly be found guilty of 'laziness'. That may be less disreputable but it will still undo a lot of the good work you've done and the good impression you've made in other respects.

2   All quotations must be (a) relevant and (b) followed through.

Quotations never speak for themselves: accompanying analysis is essential. Unadorned quotation amounts to so much empty space, and it, too, suggests laziness – someone who cannot quite be bothered to do the thing properly.

If you follow the above advice – especially that which deals with traps to avoid and the need to stay yourself – I cannot *guarantee* that you will soon develop into an attractive and persuasive writer, but I *am* pretty confident of such an outcome. You may even exemplify this wonderful description offered by Blaise Pascal:

> **When we see a natural style, we are astonished and delighted: for we expected to see an author, and we find a man.**

Now let's 'Make it'.

Chapter 6

Making it

Preliminary

> Education is a process of development and growth. And it is the process and not merely the result that is important. A truly healthy person is not fixed and completed. He is a person whose processes and activities go on in such a way that he will continue to be healthy.
>
> John Dewey

You will find plenty of people who disagree with that definition – among them sometime Chief Inspector of Schools Chris Woodhead, who argued that Dewey's works should be banned from all teacher-training institutions. And you may have doubts yourself, especially over Dewey's second sentence. You have not, presumably, worked with dedication and a considerable amount of self-sacrifice (on your part and that of others) to see the result of all those labours semi-dismissed via the adverb 'merely'. You might even be disposed to travel at least some of the way down the Woodhead road, finding Dewey's words ill-considered, unrealistic, even sentimental.

I hope it will not dismay you to learn that I am a great and unrepentant admirer of Dewey, whose above remarks seem to me as wise as they are accurate. Please look a little more carefully than I briefly encouraged you to do at that second sentence. You will see that he does *not*, in fact, imply that your result is less important than the process that led you to it, only that it is not *more* so. His definition proposes process and product as symbiotic – mutually nourishing and mutually dependent. Actually, I'd go further: without a proper awareness of and attention to process, product is necessarily compromised and invariably diminished.

That is why the previous five chapters have largely concerned themselves with process – the business of learning and developing your skills, techniques and aptitude; your week-by-week experience as you grow in knowledge and confidence; the delusions and snares you will encounter, need to recognise and then avoid; and – maybe most important of all – the lovely fact that to a serious and ambitious student, all such process is enjoyable and rewarding as well as demanding. Nevertheless, such right-minded thinking, however true, never cuts much ice with students whose results have disappointed them, especially if that means they cannot go on to do what they wanted to do. So this final chapter is about to devote itself exclusively to ensuring that you indeed 'make it' – i.e. secure the best possible product.

Before that, though, one last preliminary observation. In each of my (three) previous books on Study Skills, the section on 'examinations' was the biggest, running to well over thirty pages. This incarnation is much shorter – chiefly because I am confident that you need much less help than the readership 'targeted' in those works. One reason for that is your high calibre; another is that if you've followed and benefited from the advice provided in the previous five process chapters, the chances are very high that your product is already going to impress. But there will still be ways in which you can acquire even greater 'match fitness'. What follows may only improve your performance by 5 per cent – but that apparently modest increase is invariably crucial when you're after Straight 'A's. I hope, too, that there's an illuminating surprise or two along the way.

For the smart student, exam preparation starts long before the run-up to the papers themselves or even the final period of revision. As with most things in life, it begins by getting one's *mindset* right.

Attitudes 1: examiners – monsters, robots or humans?

> Teacher   *Examiners are just people.*
> Paranoid student *Yes, they start out that way, I've heard . . .*

Even the best and most serene students will experience an occasional stressed-out identification with those words of their 'spokesperson', but however much you might briefly warm to such waggish cynicism, it will severely hamper you if it takes root. Please get these two things into your head and keep them firmly nailed there:

- Examiners are hired to do one job and one job only: to assess whether you can do what the exam asks you to do. If you do that well, you will score well.
- Examiners *like* good scripts. They are easier and more pleasurable to read, and because of that they also earn their money faster!

Examiners aren't interested in exposing what you might fearfully think are the bottomless pits of your ignorance; instead, they will look for the small hills of erudition that they can reward. That has nothing to do with being 'nice': they can only deal with what is there, not what is not. So take comfort in those small hills; if you register enough of them, you will create enough peaks to stack up quite an impressive range.

So we can, I hope, straightaway scrub out 'monsters' from the agenda. However, before we plump absolutely for 'humans', the third option – 'robots' – needs to be investigated with some care.

I recently got into a correspondence with a bright sixteen-year-old (not a pupil at my own school) who was seeking help on how to approach exam answers, and it emerged that he'd been taught to assume that:

Examiners are stupid.

Therefore, he had further been counselled, the best plan was to trot out everything that he could, with especial emphasis on spelling out the obvious.

Initially, I was appalled. The advice struck me as deranged in theory and, judging from the bloated and repetitive essays he sent me for comment, savagely injurious in practice. Subsequently, however, I heard a much-admired colleague use exactly those three words while we were team-teaching a class of eighteen-year-olds. He immediately made it clear that by 'stupid' he did *not* mean 'thick' but 'robotic' – his point being that even the most generous, imaginative and high-powered examiner is constrained by and indeed answerable to the mark scheme of the paper at issue.

Maybe that undoubted truth was also what my correspondent's teacher had meant, causing me to wonder exactly how the sentiment had been phrased and whether the student's response was in line with what was being recommended. To put it tersely:

Was his awful strategy his fault or his teacher's?

More starkly still, I have to say that the notion that examiners are stupid in the sense of *cerebrally challenged* or *not fit for purpose* is doubly calamitous, not counting the fact that it is very rarely true.[1] First, even if you avoid 'cat sat on the mat' primitivism, you will almost certainly spell things out in excessive and laborious fashion, sacrificing tempo and the kind of snap that characterises all good answers. Second, your *tone* is likely to be not just annoying but insulting. When addressing someone you consider stupid, it is extremely difficult at the best of times not to reveal that opinion in the way you speak or write, and in an exam I'd say it's virtually impossible. You cannot afford to take that chance:

Even people who are far from mental giants know when they're being patronised, *and they hate it*.

So delete 'stupid' from your 'examiner's mindset'. There may be the odd occasion when it might have some validity, but it is a highly unsafe bet. At best the notion will sap your confidence, compromise your impetus and dilute your intellectual vigour; at worst you won't get anywhere near your true performance-level while at the same time ruinously alienating your marker.

As noted, 'robotic' is a different matter altogether. Whatever the subject or level, all examinations are governed by Assessment Criteria and an accompanying mark scheme, and examiners who wilfully sidestep such stipulations – no matter how admirable their reasons may be – will be corrected, reprimanded or even dismissed. As a high-flyer, you should not be worried or, worse, snooty about this. It does not mean that the entire enterprise is a matter of mindless 'box-ticking' or that you will not be rewarded for incisive thinking and imaginative response. After all, the award of a top grade as opposed to a significantly lower one must hinge on the former recognising superior judgement, insight and knowledge; as I hope I've persuaded you, examiners (and indeed the exam itself) are very much looking to find and acknowledge such virtues.

What it *does* mean, though, is the need to be sensible and professional as well as gifted and talented. And even if you have never thought of examiners as stupid in any sense, this 'general principle' should prove decisively beneficial:

> **Always 'take care of business'. And that includes paying proper respect to *the obvious*.**

Your answers need a good foundation just as any house does. As S.T. Coleridge unimprovably observed:

> **Poetry is certainly something more than good sense, but it must be good sense ... just as a palace is more than a house, but it must be a house.**

Your high-flying target is more a 'palace' than (say) a maisonette, but both dwellings will soon collapse if the basic cement isn't right!

In summary:

> **Respect – and *enjoy* – the obvious. And make sure you *log* it. Then you can go on to what makes you tick and what makes you special.**

Attitudes 2: priming yourself

Concerning your ideal 'performance', my first tip has been implicit in most of my advice so far. Let me now make it toughly explicit:

> **Try to imagine yourself as your marker/examiner.**

As I've pointed out, examiners prefer good candidates, so there's no need to transform yourself into a snarling masochist. But pay close and regular attention to these considerations:

• Mechanical accuracy

Sloppy spelling and punctuation can undermine even the best answers – I might say *especially* the best – so make sure those foundations are in good order.

• Clarity I: Sentence structure and expression

Are your sentences under control or are they showing signs of rambling? And are you saying what you *want* to say or *think* you're saying? You can render both questions irrelevant by *not starting a sentence till you're pretty sure how and where it's going to end.* That way you'll be in charge of all that matters.

* Clarity II: Paragraphing and 'case development'

I've said virtually everything I need to say about paragraphing in Chapter 3; all I'd add is that even terrific candidates often ignore this essential item in an exam. This may be understandable – they're under multiple pressure, they're focused on recording as much of their learning as they can and so forth – but it's still injurious. If necessary, write PARAGRAPHS in large letters on a piece of rough paper that is easily and constantly visible to you, and act on it if you've been temporarily remiss.

By 'case development' I mean the deployment of any argument, investigation or analysis. If you've obeyed the injunctions given already, it's unlikely, having been so precise about the smaller components, that you'll suddenly lurch into incoherence on a larger scale, but it can happen. Take a moment or two to check whether your work really is going in the direction you want and envisaged, or whether you're wandering.

Those three 'targets' above endorse and flesh out a tip offered in the previous chapter:

Forcibly remind yourself to look over your work as you go.

Doing so will avoid wasteful and irritating repetition, also re-sharpening your sense of direction and destination. That will make your work more pleasing to read – and that quality is as valuable in an exam as anywhere else. And you are more likely to follow this important strategy if you build it into your mindset well in advance.

Incidentally, that last tip strikes me as much more likely to be productive than one with which you are undoubtedly familiar:

Always leave yourself ten minutes at the end of the exam to check and improve what you've written.

This worthy advice is annually trotted out by teachers in their tens of thousands, and their students take due note of it, nodding wisely the while. The only trouble is that when it comes to that exam crunch:

Hardly any of them *do* it.

That may seem forgetful, perverse, even stupid; there are, in fact, a number of good reasons for such omission, and I'll be investigating them later. The 'alternative' policy of looking back over your answers *as you write* is, I think, more likely to be acted on – not least because it is highly analogous to earlier advice concerning 'regular review'. Its examination-equivalent is not difficult to implement, as I'll also be showing later.

During these pages I have observed more than once that becoming a successful student hinges as much on an awareness of what to avoid and how *not* to do it as on more 'positive' techniques; acquiring the right 'attitudes' is another case in point. Recently I heard a woman dismiss an idea she thought worthless in this splendid fashion:

I don't buy that; in fact, I wouldn't even *rent* it.

That should be your response to four matters explored earlier:

- Stop worrying about your handwriting. All that matters is that the examiner can read it without excessive effort. If your work were *truly* illegible, you'd have been told as much long ago.
- Get to know the substance and shape of your syllabuses, yes, and be sure about Attainment Objectives or whatever such things may be called in the courses you're following. *But don't fool around with any 'question-spotting' idiocy,* and if you are unfortunate enough to have a teacher who traffics in such folly, pay absolutely no attention. Devote your energies to learning, not gambling.
- Forget all bloated taught introductory structures and pompous fillers: be *you*.
- Exams are very rarely a matter of luck, of having a 'good' or 'bad' day or any similar superstitious paranoia. If you've worked sensibly and successfully during your course, the huge probability is that your exam performance and result will

fully reflect that. Repeat that as a *mantra* until it is no longer necessary.

Revision and review

In a way, that subtitle is the wrong way round. If you have taken my earlier advice, you will have become accustomed to regular review of your work, to updating your notes and ideas as you learn, and to a consequent awareness of where you are solid and where you are less so. All that should mean that your final revision is an in charge time devoted to plugging any remaining gaps, consolidating your many strengths and almost visibly increasing your confident control.

That may sound blasé on my part, especially if it crosses your mind that it's a very long time since I sat an exam, whereas you are at the climactic stage crucial to the fulfilment of your ambitions and all your efforts. I would be distressed – for *your* sake – if that was your reaction, because the last thing I intend is to encourage in you anything approaching 'It'll be all right on the night' complacency. Far from demeaning the importance of your final weeks of preparatory study and/or inviting you to be casually self-indulgent, I offer instead another 'general principle':

Effective *Review* during the *process* period guarantees decisively successful *Revision* for the ultimate *product*.

The strategy should be familiar to you from Chapter 3. Yet for all its sophistication it is founded on something utterly basic: the meaning of words.

Three definitions of revision follow. Which is correct? Or to put it another way, which one best describes your own perception and practice?

1   A second or subsequent look.
2   A new or changed look – i.e. a *reconsideration*.
3   An activity not only quite separate from other tasks but by definition *postponed* till the end of your course.

My answer (and I hope yours) is:

I and 2 are both correct and essential; 3 is a recipe for disaster.

I'll return to 1 and 2 shortly; 3 needs immediate attention, mainly because it is dangerously seductive, and for two powerful reasons:

A   In one respect it is undoubtedly true.

The climax of a course of study *does* involve the drawing together of all its strands, weaving a kind of tapestry where both the details and the overall picture are secure and convincing.

B   It is encouraged – indeed *fuelled* – by an army of adult advisers.

As the last three months of their courses loom, sons and daughters all over the world are counselled, cajoled, constrained or just plain *nagged* to 'think revision'. This is the time when, in the family home, school or college reports are pored over as never before: parents balefully recite and minutely scrutinise every last comment. The fact that all this is well-meant does not make it any less tiresome, especially as the upshot is invariably the same as I remember from my own teenage days – the 'See-here-young-man' order to spend several hours per day at one's desk.

If you think I'm exaggerating, you're lucky. For it's not just most parents who become obsessive on the subject: an uncomfortable number of teachers do as well. Those reports just mentioned teem with earnest observations about extensive revision programmes and the attendant need to devote a hefty quotient of hours to them. Well, I can help you somewhat by pointing out that report-writing is in most respects *something that needs to be seen to have been done* rather than the provision of oracular judgements: it is a conventional ritual. As a result, when writing those reports even the bravest and most imaginative teachers are to a certain extent covering themselves as much as passing on advice. That is not remotely to disparage my profession, simply to observe that such reporting tends to generate more heat than light. And while persuading your parents of those things may be impossible or not worth the hassle, at least *you* can now be clear about them.

To bring this corrective account to a close: that third definition of revision is your enemy. Equally inimical is its misconceived half-brother – the notion that revision is an exclusively *quantitative* matter. In spite of a Himalayan amount of evidence to the contrary, far too many adults preach this doctrinal equation:

**The number of hours expended is in direct proportion
to progress and chances of decisively increased success.**

To put it kindly, that is a seriously inaccurate myth; a less tactful
summary would be

Toxic nonsense.

It's not just that it isn't true: as I trust is evident by now, it
leads to activity that is misplaced and wasteful, and thus
damaging. There is only one situation where sheer time-expendi-
ture matters: when the student is in effect starting from scratch,
having failed to absorb the requisite information and knowledge
along the way. That isn't revision but 'remedial re-learning' –
something I cannot imagine an aspirant high-flyer needing to do
at any stage, let alone the final one.

Enough of the negative and the dangerous: time to concentrate
on the best ways to go about your final preparation. I strongly
advise you to:

• Work in short, intense bursts.

I'm not going to be *time-precise* about these, and nor should you
be: to repeat, your concentration spans (a) are unique and (b) will
vary according to time of day, the topic being studied and several
other factors However, bearing in mind four 'will to work' components encountered in Chapter 3 should enable you to manage
your time in productive and satisfying fashion:

1 Specific goals (content)   *What* we want to do
2 Intensity   *How much* we want to do
3 Times   *When* we want to work
4 Duration   *How long* we want to work.

Those observations are general principles informing your entire
revision period. These next two tips should be acted on *at its
outset.*

• First: look over *all* your work during the course.

That means all your notes (including, I trust, revisionist updates);
all your assignments, and your teachers' comments on them, be

they corrections or further 'food for thought'; anything you've downloaded from the Net or researched in pulped-tree publications; in short, *everything you've done*.

•   Next: identify your weaknesses or gaps.

There won't be many of these, but no matter how gifted you are and however conscientious you've been, there will be *some*. Make them your priority. Yes, it's hard to focus first on those inadequacies about which you'd rather not be reminded, but it's an unimprovable policy. You'll be doing it at your freshest, and if you make even half the progress I'd expect you to do, you will have the satisfaction that comes from 'taking care of business' – especially as this particular business is your nastiest.

My penultimate observations in this section return us to the two 'correct' definitions of revision outlined above. Little additional time need be spent on no. 1. If you have practised regular review of your work, you will have taken maybe six 'subsequent looks' at it – and that ought already to guarantee its place in your long-term memory, those few remaining gaps duly acknowledged. But don't skimp that seventh or final look: regard it as an ideal opportunity to engage definition no. 2, 'reconsideration'.

Your knowledge and understanding are now at their peak, and much greater than they were six months or a year ago. That increase is not just a matter of detail: your awareness of 'the bigger picture' will be both sharper and deeper. As a result, fresh ideas are likely to come to you, broadening your scope and strengthening your control. Such new insights or 'takes' are pleasing experiences, too, and they also boost your confidence – always important as you approach any kind of crunch.

Two final brief injunctions:

•   Take plenty of rest.
•   Have a good time.

Being 'match-fit' for exams is emphatically not just a matter of exercising and cramming your brain. Answering questions under multiple pressure requires energy, stamina and calm nerves; these are far more likely to be 'on stream' if your body is rested and relaxed and your mind serene. In the large majority of cases, happy students tend to be successful ones, so make sure the Pleasure Principle is properly in evidence during that last lap.

In the exam hall

First, let's make doubly sure you're going in with the right attitude.

Exams are conservative mechanisms. Their purpose is not to catch you out but straightforwardly to test what you know and how you think. They are not perfect mechanisms, admittedly, but they are thoughtfully composed and even more carefully marked. It is only the naive cynic or the terrified inadequate who regard them as cruel lotteries.

For any good student, an exam is a 'you and them' *partnership*: you show your quality, they reward it. And if you find that analysis on the rosy side, it's still a lot more accurate than 'It's me against them' paranoia. Banish such fearful thoughts at once and for all.

Nevertheless, all examination candidates – including the brightest and most thoroughly accomplished – face one potential hazard, and it is an extreme one.

Danger of death: the first two minutes

During my stern observations earlier about sloppily written emails, I quoted the Latin motto *festina lente* (see p. 58). At no time is that 'hurry slowly' advice more crucially important than at the start of an exam.

That has always been true; however, it is much harder to act on than when I sat exams thirty-plus years ago. If I remember rightly (and I'm confident that I do) Sir Chief Invigilator intoned just the one remark:

You may now open your exam paper and begin writing.

These days the start of an exam is a protracted affair, not to mention buttock-clenchingly tedious and enraging in more or less equal measure. From Alaska to Zambia, examinees are subjected to a litany of instructions, almost all of them of a 'Thou shalt not' complexion. To that can be added the surrender of mobile phones; ditto any 'open book' texts whose (scholarly) annotation might incur the disqualifying wrath of any Inspector who might happen to visit; and in certain subjects 'wiping' calculator checks.

All that adds up to (if you're fortunate) at least three minutes, and by the time those are over, you are likely to be almost murderously eager to get on with what you're there for – i.e. *doing* the exam rather than being harangued about its sanctity.

That entirely understandable urge *must* be resisted.

The actual start of your exam time is exactly the same as it was for mine – when Sir Chief Invigilator[2] gives you the go-ahead to begin strutting your stuff.

It is often said that 'Exam Rule no. 1' is:

Do what you're told.

I agree with the sentiment but it should be Rule *Two*. As Rule One I nominate:

Do not write a word on your answer booklet until you are sure of what the question is asking you to do.

In Chapter 4 I spoke of the validity of first impressions, and their worth is increased when you're responding to something that you know about.[3] In this exam context, however, they are not enough, however reliable they might subsequently turn out to be. You cannot afford to be quick or instinctive: check every last component of the question, and then check it again. Above all, to return to a matter already covered twice (see pp. 17–18 and 118–19):

Decode all the relevant *command verbs*.

Then, and only then, you can start writing.

Good students rarely underachieve in exams because they have not prepared well enough or been poorly taught. They do so because they misread questions, rush into things prematurely, go off at tangents, or all three. So this section's subtitle is not melodramatic: getting it wrong in those first two minutes really will kill off your chances of a top grade.

Now on to something that may be less lethal but can still crucially dilute your performance.

Danger of dissolution: pacing yourself and staying alert

Exams vary in duration. Some are over in just forty-five minutes; there are a few that last for three hours. The norm, however, is ninety minutes or two hours, and I would guess those figures will apply to most of the papers you sit. And the first thing to say is that working under great pressure for that long is:

Decidedly unusual, even *unnatural*.

That is not something I would want you to *worry* about. Everybody involved in exams, from setters to markers to final awarders, recognises this property, and allowance for it is built in to every paper.

However, it is something you should take due and proper note of, for that should help you deploy your time to maximum effect. If it *is* 'unnatural' to work unrelievedly for such a period, then:

Don't do it!

In one respect, two hours in an exam is like two hours anywhere else: it is a *dynamic*. Your rhythms and energy levels vary, as does your concentration and physical awareness, including comfort, the need for brief refreshment and so on. Those things *are* natural, indeed basic; so go with and act on them. As the English idiom has it:

A change is as good as a rest.

Having a brief stretch or a slug of water not only refreshes you *physically*: the change of activity sharpens the brain and the psyche. And if you feel like taking the odd chill-out rest, that too is perfectly in order.

Healthy in themselves (though don't overdo them!), those 'off-duty moments' dramatise an important truth which can be applied in more active ways:

You do not have to write all the time, nor should you do so.

It is not only *sensible* to spend a minute or two reflecting or planning further: it is *essential*. If you career headlong through your answer at the handwriting equivalent of ninety miles per hour, a lot of bad things are going to happen:

- Your paragraphing and other design features will be either non-existent or seriously flawed.
- Your sentences and structures will be less coherent than they might or should be.
- You are almost certainly going to repeat yourself, possibly several times over.
- Your material will be unselective and therefore lack bite, even judgement. A good answer does not comprise wholesale unconsidered regurgitation.
- Your work will tend to be shapeless, or at any rate blurred.

Those shortcomings will not mean that you *fail*; they will, however, make that top grade very unlikely.

So *pace* your efforts and *stay fully in touch* with your work. The best way to do both returns us to two ideas mentioned earlier in this chapter:

From time to time, check over what you've written.

This is not a difficult habit to acquire, and it has three major strengths:

1   It gives you a break – not the same as an actual rest, but just as valuable.
2   It is very likely to trigger new ideas and/or remind you of those in your head when you began.
3   It allows you to correct any errors or clumsiness – including the provision of overlooked paragraphing! – while you're still freshly aware of what you've written. Doing it now is immeasurably more productive than attempting it at the very end.

That last sentence reactivates what I will call 'The last ten minutes controversy'. As noted, countless teachers advise their students to safeguard that time for thorough checking; also as noted, very few students actually do it. And here I think their practice is superior to the advice they've received, which is self-evidently unrealistic and also unsound, both physically and psychologically.

There are some examinees who do come to a natural close shortly before the order to 'stop writing'. But there aren't many of them, and my hunch is that *very* few of them are high-flyers. Those students invariably have a great deal to say, perhaps more than time allows, and they almost automatically decide to use their final moments to log new material rather than edit what they've already done. And while it is probably true that an extra couple of paragraphs or points are unlikely to make that much difference to the final mark, try telling that to a student who is 'on a roll' and determined to finish with a flourish.

Moreover, editing at the end of a lengthy and intense period of work is hardly ever effective, whether in an exam hall or at one's desk. The brain is buzzing, the body fatigued – a far from ideal combination when the objective is cool, self-critical alertness. Besides and finally, if you've got into the habit of reviewing your exam work as you go, that final check should not be necessary anyway.

The longest day: wall-to-wall exams

All over the world, examination boards and authorities try – they really do! – to make life as comfortable as they can for their candidates. However, because of the profusion of subjects on offer and the number of papers they embrace, examination timetables are becoming increasingly crowded, even grid-locked, and the ideal scenario of 'morning on, afternoon off' (or vice versa) is not always possible. This section is designed to help you to cope with the prospect of three or four exams in a single day. The model I have chosen is a current UK one, but the strategies proposed should prove beneficial wherever you are and whatever your level.

For at least three years, any seventeen-year-old UK student taking English Literature and Geography has sat those papers – all *four* of them – on the same day.

1 The English papers take place during the morning – first Shakespeare and then Poetry and Prose. Each lasts ninety minutes; candidates are given a fifteen-minute break in between.
2 Less than two hours later, those students will sit two Geography papers (identical timings and arrangements).
3 In sum: six hours of intense and intensive work between 09.15 and 16.00.

I don't know about you, but just thinking about all that makes me feel tired. And the trouble doesn't stop there.

4   Those two English papers demand not just stamina but a forbidding degree of intellectual gymnasticism. In the space of three hours, students have to focus on a seventeenth-century drama and then (say) a nineteenth-entury novel and a twentieth-century poet.
5   The Geography papers are similarly wide-ranging, engaging a host of different skills and approaches. In addition, those candidates will already be feeling jaded even at the start.

Significantly, if paradoxically, the danger is greatest at the *start* of such a day, not in the afternoon (that 'jaded' factor notwithstanding). By 15.00 the Geography candidates can reflect that the worst, or at any rate most, is over, and that can trigger a burst of energy that results in some impressive work. But those same students at 9.15, despite being fresh and focused, may well feel daunted by the vista of hours stretching out before them, thus finding it hard to focus or just get going.

You might think that sounds fanciful, but a survey of the performances of such candidates over the three years in question suggests otherwise. In a telling number of cases, candidates' worst performance was on the Shakespeare paper. Now, it could be that there were other reasons for that – less effective teaching than for the other texts; the students' lack of sympathy for Shakespeare or the difficulties his work poses. However, I think it extremely unlikely that the disappointing results of *all* those examinees – from many schools and centres, studying different plays – can be explained in such a way. The 'Longest Day' factor is much more probable.

How to combat it? Well, just reading these last few paragraphs should get you half way. A problem is always reduced and more manageable for it being anticipated; if you find yourself faced with such an indecently packed exam day, make a special effort to be on form from the beginning. Don't dwell on the hours to come: take care of each piece of business as you go. Taking note of those examination dynamics will assist you in that respect; so will the positive reflection that by the end of that day, you'll have completed a hefty proportion of your exam time!

Conclusion

This chapter has largely centred on attitudes and mental strategies. Advice on such practical considerations as planning, performance techniques, writing introductions and conclusions, stating one's terms, coping with multiple-choice papers and other such technical matters has either been provided earlier or (in keeping with my governing assumption that you are highly equipped go-getters) strike me as surplus to your requirements. If you require further help in such things, the Bibliography should aid you. All I want to add is:

Enjoy yourself!

One of this book's earliest observations was that enjoyment is not just a matter of pleasure but of savouring victory. I hope that *Getting Straight 'A's* has ensured that you experience both kinds, and to the full.

Appendix I

Net practice

I've made more than a few references to the Internet in the course of this book, but I have not devoted a section of any substance to it. That is because you almost certainly know more about it than I. In the last five years or so, the Net has become the student's main and most immediate research source; as a result, when it comes to website knowledge, efficient use of search engines and sheer technological facility, young users have left most of their teachers standing. Indeed, I have already learnt a good deal about such things from my own students, who in this instance are the professionals while I'm the amateur. On the assumption that you resemble them in that respect, I'm not going to waste any time telling you things you know already and better than I.

However, I do want not so much to sound a note of warning as offer two positive though cautionary tips. The first hinges on two observations.

1   The *best* thing about the Net is that it is democratic.

Naturally, many properties of the Net are worth celebrating. Five that spring instantly to my mind are:

- Access to a world of information available without you having to move out of your chair, let alone out of the house.
- The sheer speed with which you can engage that facility.
- Being able to download desired material simply, quickly and cheaply. The previous alternatives were either laborious and slow (writing the text out by hand) or cumulatively very expensive (using a photocopier).

- eBay and all such similar hunting, buying and selling facilities.
- The Net is enormous *fun*. Computers and the Net enable any number of serious activities and achievements, but they are also wondrous *toys*. Provided that attribute is not idly indulged, it is a decisively enabling factor for any student: pleasure always is.

Yet those five and the host of others like them are, finally, *relative*. They may be superior to the old ways and research-procedures (which, after all, is what 'progress' is supposed to mean and involve) but they deal with the same needs and desires which have characterised inquisitive minds since the dawn of civilisation. We are talking about a difference in degree, not in kind.

The *democratic* nature of the Internet is, however, a unique historical phenomenon. Until its instigation, to get anything published meant submitting it to someone, who would then give either the thumbs-up or the thumbs-down.[1] No matter whether the work in question was of earth-shattering significance, worthily important, or abject drivel, the driving criterion was 'economics'. In the vast majority of instances, that meant money and only money, ranging from the nervous wish to cover one's costs to the Eldorado of a global best-seller. Occasionally, the economic concern was more to do with staying alive than making money, i.e. publishing something that would enrage and therefore make one a target.[2] But whatever the precise nature of those economics, one fact was constant for all authors, whether would-be, quietly established or hugely successful:

Somebody other than you had to say 'Yes'.

No longer so. Anybody can set up a website; that same anybody can therefore – barring certain legal constraints[3] – publish on it anything s/he wants to.

And this is wonderful. It means that the 'ordinary person' has been *truly* empowered, not condescendingly pandered to by such cheap (in both senses) pretences as the phone-in programme, the email-response to newspaper articles, media websites and the like. Those are all variants on 'Letters to *The Times*', which may briefly gratify the published writer but beyond that do little or no significant *work*. The Internet is in its infancy, but as it develops into adolescence and then maturity, the possibilities for all our voices to be truly heard are excitingly increased.

If that last paragraph strikes you as suspiciously romantic, I have to say that I agree with you. For my second observation is this:

2   The *worst* thing about the Net is that it is democratic.

If absolutely anyone can publish stuff on the Net, then it is inevitable that the medium will contain more than its fair share of rubbish.[4] I'm not talking about the many, varied and repellent nastinesses that can (all too easily) be accessed; I'm talking about

Stuff that may be 'innocent' but is simply *no good*.

Early on in this book I argued that plagiarism is not just a vice but enormously dangerous to any student. Now I will go further:

There is only one thing worse than plagiarism: *stupid* plagiarism.

If you *insist* on lifting stuff and passing it off as your own, then at least make sure that what you're stealing is worth the risk.

I am being both facetious and deadly serious. Of course I am not suggesting that cunning plagiarism is a good idea, either practically or morally. But I am saying that even if your Net-searching motives are as pure as could be, your judgement must from start to finish be in charge. So when zapping websites, you need to bear in mind these criteria in terms of the material's reliability and/or whether you trust it:

1   Who wrote it? Have you heard of the author? If not, are you able to find out about him/her?

The search engines will quickly assist that quest; other productive checking-sources include reference books, libraries and your teachers.

2   Does the text make sense to you? Is it plausible?
3   Is it balanced, or pursuing an obvious 'line' or evident bias?
4   How well is it written? Are the mechanics accurate?

If not, be immediately suspicious: you will, I hope, recall my earlier observation that a writer who can't be bothered to take care of the little things is invariably no less indifferent to and sloppy about the big ones.

5   Even if the text is flawlessly correct, how do you respond to its style and tone?

If it displeases or troubles you, be no less suspicious.

6   How does it fit in with what you know already? If it doesn't, are these new ideas exciting and revelatory, or do they seem dodgy?
7   What is the website's purpose? Is it truly educational, or is it trying to *sell* you something, either literally or metaphorically?

Either way, be *very* wary of such mercenary 'pitches'.

8   Finally, to expand no. 1: can you cross-reference the text with other authorities and material, so as to confirm or negate its reliability?

Naturally, all those questions and your response to them should also characterise your research in other media. But since the Net is very likely to be your main source, you should engage it with caution as well as justified enthusiasm. It is still excitingly new, it has immense charm and seemingly awesome potency – and those properties can disarm you in a fashion not entirely dissimilar from how a cobra mesmerises its prey. That's why I used the phrase 'deadly serious' just now: trusting the Net *regardless* will not of course kill you, but it could kill off your chances of top-flight success.

One last piece of advice. If you are writing an assignment of any kind, or even if you're making detailed notes Word documents and the like, try if possible to:

Get away from the Net, email and every other 'extra' PC facility.

While writing these selfsame pages, I found myself regularly breaking off to check emails or visit my Net 'Favourites'. Okay, perhaps I was getting tired or just running short of juice, but it was still not a very bright way to take care of business. Try not to be as dumb as me! If that assignment, draft essay or preliminary note-taking is important to you, tear yourself away – even if it's only a matter of a few feet – from the PC and use a laptop or palm-computer; if neither is available to you, you'll just have to find more willpower than I have usually been able to exert. In bygone times, writers used to work in a room where there was no phone and, better still, no chance of hearing it elsewhere in the house when it rang. Ignoring the blandishments of the Internet and email housed in the machine you're currently using to write is considerably more difficult, but if you want those straight 'A's, you will need at times to find a way to do it.

Appendix II

Noting exercise (Chapter 5)

*This is my 'notional model answer' to the exercise that appears on pp. 115–16. You may disagree with some of my choices/priorities, which is your right and privilege. My main hope is that what follows is not too difficult to decipher in its multiple typeface **and that my reasons for designating material according the 1, 2, 3 or 4 code below are clear.***

<u>Bold underlined</u>	1	Utterly fundamental material
Bold	2	Primary/essential material
Ordinary type	3	Secondary material
Italics	4	Merely illustrative or ultimately marginal material

ELVIS PRESLEY'S SYMBOLIC DECLINE

The story of Elvis Presley is one that is not only both tragic and tacky but also decisively, almost symbolically, American. **<u>When he burst on the scene in the mid-1950s, Presley was a talent as shocking for some as he was exciting for others,</u>** full of a raw power whose sexuality was almost tangible. (*Within months, any below-waist shots of Elvis performing were banned on US TV and newsreel.*) He drew on the separate-yet-linked traditions of hillbilly music and the blues, a potent combination made all the more exciting by **a voice at once true and husky and a rhythmic flair that no other mass-selling artist has ever approached.** And to quote one of his 1958 hits, Elvis was 'Trouble'. In an America gripped by the Cold-War-dominated ethos of the Eisenhower years *and for whom McCarthyism was still an issue,* the youthful rebellion and sheer energy that Presley embodied were not only alarming but indecent to the point of un-Americanness. Marxism was, in Robert Hughes's phrase, 'America's nurturing enemy', and anything or anyone who diverted the nation's zeal from focusing on the 'Red Menace' was bad news – 'trouble' in abundance.

Some of you may have an idea of what happened next. Presley remained a 'dangerous', youth-oriented singer for another two or so years, *during which time he had an unbroken string of hits that mined further the earthiness of his first records, e.g. Jailhouse Rock, I Got Stung, Big Hunk Of Love* and *Hard-Headed Woman. Even while America's young was rocking and rolling to such joyous and seemingly anarchic sounds, though,* a softening-up process was going on. **Colonel Tom Parker, Presley's manager, had already determined that Elvis would become an all-round family entertainer**, for reasons that had as much to do with small-town conservative values as with money. (*For Parker, the two things were intimately related, if not synonymous.*) **In 1958 Presley went into the army.** Unsurprisingly (it must now be said) he emerged as the model soldier, all modest dutifulness and artful (that is to say coached) gung-ho patriotism. **By the time he was demobbed, middle – and** *middle-aged* **– America had already taken him to their hearts**, and Parker's long-term plan streamrollered into action.

For a while there were still glimpses of the 'old' Elvis – *songs like Stuck On You, Such A Night, Feel So Bad, Good Luck Charm, and the 1963 Devil In Disguise, which in the view of many was his very last rock record of true quality.* **But these were mixed up with and into a schmaltz of increasing remorselessness** – *Are You Lonesome Tonight?, the cringingly devout Crying In The Chapel* and – *an all too significant title* – *Sentimental Me.* **At the same time his conveyor-belt movies accelerated in both frequency and lousiness.** Initially Elvis had been a striking actor (very powerful in *King Creole*, based on Harold Robbins's *A Stone For Danny Fisher*, and also impressive in *Jailhouse Rock* and *Flaming Star*), but now his every cinematic outing was an exercise in semi-idiocy, occasionally alleviated by the odd good song.

Grimly eloquent is this information unearthed in 2002 by Glyn Brown: 'Shockingly, we discover that Presley was offered parts in Midnight Cowboy, West Side Story, the Kris Kristofferson role in A Star Is Born *– which he begged to do but the percentage wasn't high enough for the Colonel.* Instead, we had Elvis in Fun In Acapulco *(playing a sea-going trapeze artist),* in Harum Scarum, *in* Girls, Girls, Girls.' *Brown gleaned this from* Elvis: By Those Who Knew Him Best *by Rose Clayton and Dick Heard (Virgin), one of two new books on Presley reviewed in Brown's article for* The Times *in July 2002.*

Many commentators argue that Presley enjoyed a revival in the 1970s. That may have been true commercially, but it is hard to see his recordings of that time as anything but a pale, crowd-pleasing shadow of his earlier work. That astonishing voice remained more or less unimpaired to the end, but his rhythmic sense became almost as sluggish as his increasingly bloated physique, and he was no more exciting than other middle-aged survivors *such as Tom Jones and Englebert Humperdink. Unlike them, though,* Presley did not survive for very long. His increasingly destructive, even insane lifestyle took its ultimate toll in the summer of 1977, when Elvis died. He was forty-two.

Nor is it easy to understand why his appeal and iconic status remain undimmed nearly thirty years on. The still-electric quality of his early records may partly explain it; yet the 'Elvis Lives!' clan – and it's a very big clan – celebrate <u>everything</u> he recorded with the same uncritical devotion. Perhaps one answer lies in Presley's definitive American-ness. <u>A once-thrilling, wondrously energetic and original talent all too rapidly descended into sentimentality, sterile economics and, ultimately, sanctimonious self-destruction. The story of Elvis furnishes a disturbing model of America itself.</u>

Notes

Chapter 1 Naming it

1 This is not the place to discuss Tony Blair's still-theoretical vision of a graduate democracy, but its wisdom seems at least questionable. Many educationalists doubt both its appropriateness and its chances of working properly; several of my acquaintance consider the idea simply mad.

2 Results have unbrokenly 'got better' for at least twenty years. This is ludicrous on any basis other than selective reference-normed statistics, and it surprises me that anyone takes the claim seriously any more.

3 With the at least partial exception of the International Baccalaureate, about which I shall be making a number of observations during this book.

4 Despite the sceptical, sometimes downright crabby remarks above, I would not number current Western incarnations among that description. Even the most superficially passing acquaintance with programmes favoured at every educational level by Nazi Germany, the 1917–92 USSR and certain other regimes still very much with us demonstrates two things. One, however bad things may look to certain Western eyes, we have yet to get anywhere near plumbing those depths. Two, those horrific programmes *did not work,* i.e. they failed to stop people thinking, wanting something better for their minds, bodies and spirits. George Orwell was, thank goodness, utterly wrong about that in his still-absurdly oversung *1984,* and unless and until Mogadon Man comes to rule the earth – and I mean *all* of it – he always will be.

5 No Board can afford to set these – they would cause mayhem among its own examiners; in addition, doing so would threaten the 'ever upwards' graph of improvement, which would never do.

6 If you're interested, this quaint habit owes its origins to the impulse to placate Pan, the Greek God of the Forest.

7 Quoted in Francis Wheen's *Guardian* column, 3 January, 1996.

8 Be careful about this concept, however. Sheer good luck or bad luck is far less common than many suppose.

9 Both of which I was expecting: the session was billed as catering for 'The Gifted and Talented', which was eminently the case.

10 So much so that I chose to abandon my 'set spiel' on them and move on to other things; students do not appreciate having their time wasted, especially on a Saturday!

11 This is usually referred to as SPAG, standing for Spelling, Punctuation and Grammar. In view of its absurdly under-weighted status, the acronym might perhaps be more honestly arranged as GAPS, or even GASP. In any event, the maximum amount of credit for this fundamental aspect of communication and 'business English correctness' (which everyone, everywhere requires or will require) is 5 per cent.

12 I will now, though: it is an alarming and unwise portrait of examiners with which to furnish the young, and I deal with it in full measure in Chapter 6.

13 If you're put out by these warlike images of mine, I apologise; however, I would still maintain they are all too apposite. Education-speak nowadays makes frequent and almost unthinking use of such military terms as 'targets', 'bullet points', 'tasks', 'assignments', 'objectives' and 'cohort', and for all my dislike of such practice, it gets harder not to be influenced by it, or at least respond in kind.

14 In effect, the UK Government's educational watchdog and enforcer.

15 As happened in England to a man not unlike Hitler in some respects: Oswald Mosley, the leader of the British Fascists.

16 Bernie Ohls in *The Long Goodbye* (1953, Penguin), edition, p. 238.

17 Judith Woolf, *From Notepad to Mousepad* (Routledge, 2004).

Chapter 2 Using it

1 It seems to me there is nothing to be said in favour of 'envy'. It starts off sour and usually gets worse; in extreme cases it leads the envier to wish, passionately, that s/he were someone else – one of the quickest ways to go mad. Envy is fundamentally sulky and self-pitying, as damaging to the victim as it is wholly unappealing. It could be argued that to envy someone in a spirit of desired emulation can be healthily motivating, but to my mind such a response has crossed into 'admiration', leaving envy behind.

2 The contrast with envy could not be starker – another reason why I consider the latter to be the 'odd one out'.

3 As proverbial a 'vice' as gluttony, lust or your new friend (I hope) vanity.

4 Maybe more so: a sizeable proportion of his Athenian contemporaries were *slaves* – scarcely the ideal context in which to 'be yourself'.

Chapter 3 Sorting it

1 That is, incidentally, why the school timetable has not varied in terms of standard lesson-length for over a century.

2 Such perusal may – sometimes should – include updating your notes. See Chapter 5 for chapter and verse on this important practice.

3 My metaphor comparing your brain to an engine irresistibly calls to mind the Internet 'Search Engines', which are increasingly fundamental to any student's work and research. See Chapter 5 and also Appendix I.

4 Add: 'tedious, unscientific – i.e. solely based on anecdote, prejudice or both – and about as illuminating as Blackpool's Golden Mile during a power-cut.'

5 And the *bags* in which said stuff is carted: they are *enormous*. Furthermore, many quite young pupils shoulder two such, the combined avoirdupois of which rivals their own body weight.

6 As noted earlier, though, do yourself an intellectually beneficial and money-saving favour by having nothing to do with Study Aids.

7 Does anyone hate that horribly modish phrase as much as I do? It is blandly deceptive – it includes loved ones and enemies, team-mates and rivals, those you can understand and those who seem to come from another planet. It obscures far more than it illuminates, and it might even be said that it is ultimately meaningless.

8 The term is both ugly and faintly comic; on the other hand, it identifies an important and enabling truth, which is presumably why it's survived for over thirty years.

9 The wildly contrasting sounds of Heavy Metal and a seventy-piece symphony orchestra are not a very good idea, for example. In addition, avoid music that distracts you for any other reason; it's wise to choose things that you know well and make you happy, or at least contented. Bach, Mozart and trio jazz are often cited as ideal in this respect; however, you will know best what suits you, so as with everything else, act on it.

10 C.A. Mace, *The Psychology of Study* (London: Methuen, 1932). Pelican edition (1964), p. 81.

11 The term is Rudyard Kipling's, in his enchanting 'The Elephant's Child' in *Just So Stories*.

12 If by any chance you *do* need some assistance in any of these areas, there are a number of reliable guides – including a couple of my own – listed in the Bibliography.

13 This is occurring more and more in the communications and work of the otherwise literate and bright. It looks – and *is* – indescribably idiotic, and you must never allow it to contaminate your own writing.

14 In his splendid *Full Marks* (Routledge, 2005), John Kirkman quotes from Cleanth Brooks and Robert Penn Warren's *Modern Rhetoric* to define the principal function of paragraphing as enabling a writer 'to make his thought structure visible upon the page itself'.

15 That said and fully meant, students submitting essays *must* provide generous margins, so as to allow proper space for their marker to comment, advise and discuss.

16 Not excluding Radio 4's *Today*. Along with many millions, I enjoy and largely admire this 'flagship' programme; on the other hand,

I do sometimes wonder why presenters, editors and communications gurus assume that human beings' concentration-span on any one item is five minutes maximum.

17 Just think of how many kilos of junk mail the average household gets in a week, via letter box or hidden within papers and magazines.

18 In my view, 12 is ideal. For anything in excess of 200 words, 10 makes for a demanding read, while 14 can become cumulatively hectoring. On no account go below 10 – which many students do. Such minimalism really will undermine your impact.

19 In this instance, I use 'grammar' to denote *all* mechanical skills – spelling, punctuation, paragraphing and design.

Chapter 4 Nailing it

1 'Inscrutable' comes from the same root as the verb 'scrutinise', and it means incapable of being deciphered or indeed *read*.

2 E. H. Carr, *What is History?* (London: Penguin, 1987), p.12.

3 Ibid. p. 23.

4 *The Deer Park* (André Deutsch, 1957).

5 Slightly adapted from the version supplied in the *National Literacy Strategy Framework for Teaching*, 1998.

6 A translation of the original Latin phrase *mas occasionatus*, coined by St Thomas Aquinas. He was about as far from an idiot as it's possible to be, which makes his opinion and 'proof' even more disturbing.

7 William James, *Pragmatism* (Washington Square Press, [1906] 1963). The innovative university was Edinburgh.

8 Henri Poincaré, *La Science et l'hypothèse* (1902).

9 Francis Wheen, 'The Demolition Merchants of Reality', *How Mumbo Jumbo Conquered The World* (Fourth Estate, 2004), pp. 102–3.

10 The apparently forbidding word *paradigm* is actually a straightforward concept, albeit large: it has been well defined as 'A mental construction by which we organise our reasoning and classify our knowledge' (Nicholas Alchin, *Theory of Knowledge,* John Murray, 2003), p. 169).

11 It occurs to me to add that any such figure *requiring* proof should be not only avoided but jettisoned. I am of the view that the testing of Abraham in *Genesis* (Chapter 22) is the most hideous story in the entire Old Testament, and it's not as if there isn't some strong competition. On a less extreme but still loathsome level, any 'beloved' who asks you to perform a feat of some kind to prove your love should be dumped at once. Life is too short: find someone nicer, saner and capable of emotions other than tyrannical egomania.

12 'God's Utility Function', *River Out Of Eden*. Two paragraphs later Dawkins quotes these sombre lines by the poet A.E. Housman:

> *For nature, heartless, witless Nature*
> *Will neither care nor know.*

13 Persuasively but not definitively, though: can you think of any other distinct type(s)? You'll find two more of my devising on pp. 36–7.
14 Two questions in this area might be 'Which is Shakespeare's greatest play?' or 'What is the most attractive wallpaper?'
15 Participants in any such 'debate' – be the topic violence, sex or anything that supposedly influences behaviour – would do well to consider these remarks by Clive James:

> The assumption that ordinary people's lives could be controlled and limited by what entertained them was always too condescending to be anything but fatuous. ... People don't get their their morality from their reading matter: they bring their morality to it.

> ('Princess Daisy', 1993).

16 Numbers 2 and 3 here not only qualify as 'hasty generalisations' but also futher illustrate the unwisdom of *prediction*.
17 The original illustration drawn on here concluded differently: 'my parents will be furious if you don't'. I have changed it because, it seems to me, the original could be interpreted as a *threat* rather than as an appeal to *pity*.
18 The phrase has a disreputable cousin much favoured by politicians. Next time you hear someone say, 'We have made it absolutely clear ... ,' get ready to listen to something that is either obscure, or just that moment made up, or is both so complicated and controversial that few people have any idea what the true position might be.
19 All four are also examples of generalisations which while not *apparently* 'hasty' – they are invariably delivered with considered, almost biblical weight – are so dubious as to be worthless.
20 I apologise for the impersonal style here – scarcely appropriate for such a painful mini-saga! But not for the first time, politics and language end up as enemies, or certainly in conflict. To protect gender equality when using pronouns may be politically admirable, but the now-standard insistence on such forms as *s/he, him/her, himself/herself* causes grammatical inelegance at the best of times, let alone (as is the case here) writing which is drenched in pronouns.
21 The sign was invented by Robert Recorde and appeared in his *Whetstone of Witte*, 1557. He was tiring of writing out *which is the equal of* time after time, and devised the '=' symbol on the principle that 'noe 2 things can be more equal'. His device has much in common with that valuable punctuation point, the 'colon', in that both are human inventions which sharpen meaning and save a lot of time.
22 The citing of *instruction* provides one answer to the final question heading this exercise concerning 'other types of reason'. Such further possibilities as *wish-fulfilment* and *desire for reassurance* have been implicit in my Commentary, and no doubt you've thought of others yourself. The field is very evidently a large one!
23 Coleridge once declared, 'No man does anything from a single motive', and experience suggests that in the overwhelming majority of instances he was right.

24 As a kind of postscript to Berkeley's deranged world-picture, you might wish to be alerted to one of the most (in)famous 'posers' in philosophy: 'Does the tree in the quadrangle exist when there is nobody around to see it?' You'll have guessed that Berkeley's answer was 'Yes: God perceives it.' Among alternative responses, you might favour 'Please don't waste my short time on earth with such drivel' or 'Well of *course* it ******* does.' Stuff like that makes Ambrose Bierce's sardonic definition in his *The Devil's Dictionary* (Bloomsbury, 2003) seem all too accurate:
Philosophy (n): A route of many roads leading from nowhere to nothing.

25 Other culprits include 'Fair words butter no parsnips' (you don't say); 'Still waters run deep' (they don't run *at all*, idiot: that's why they're still); 'Don't let the grass grow under your feet' (how could it possibly do that when competing with a hefty pair of Doc Martens topped by ten-stone-plus of human flesh and bone?).

26 From 'Jeeves and the Chump Cyril', *The Inimitable Jeeves* (Herbert Jenkins).

27 *The Psychology of Study*, p. 30. As noted earlier, Mace wrote his book in 1932, and his style is more cautious than I think it would be were he composing the selfsame material now. So don't be fooled by the apparent moderation of 'eccentric': I have no doubt that he meant 'as near to mad as made no difference'.

28 'Obituary of Francis Crick OM'; *Daily Telegraph*, Friday, 30 July, 2004; the italics are mine.

29 Adapted from a remark by Philip Marlowe, Raymond Chandler's greatest creation. He was talking about chess.

Chapter 5 Doing it

1 These, also known as 'Creative Patterns' or 'Brainstorming', seem to have become thoroughly tiresome to virtually all students of my acquaintance. If so, it is a sad but salutary instance of how an originally vibrant idea can be done to death. The technique has been shoved down so many contemporary students' throats since their primary school days that it has become not just stale but rotten.
   Incidentally, the term 'brainstorming' never struck me as appropriate anyway to an activity that hinges on focused planning, and now it has fallen foul of the Politically Correct Police, who think it could offend those who suffer from epilepsy.

2 Both 'cannibalised' passages here first appeared in my *Brain Train* (E & FN Spon, 1984).

3 Myalgic Encephalomyelitis, sometimes alternatively termed Chronic Fatigue Syndrome (CFS).

4 Not so long ago many people scoffed at RSI, deeming it the imaginings of the hypochondriac or the work shy. I am happy to say, however, that such dismissive scepticism has largely disappeared, and that not only have therapeutic treatments been devised to help existing

sufferers but significant advances have been made in how to diagnose and even prevent its invasion.

5 Paradox: a seemingly absurd but on reflection well-grounded and illuminating statement.

6 No more than an hour a week, probably less, especially once you're into it as a regular activity. Moreover, it's a good thing to do at the end of a fierce work-session, using the brain's residual energy before full 'turn-off' arrives. See Chapter 3.

7 'Elvis Remembered: A Gifted White-Trash Boy Who Trusted The Wrong People', *The Times* 2, 31 July, 2002.

8 Essentially the same as 'Contrast', but the separate words need to be fully registered.

9 The late Sir Kingsley Amis once observed, 'The price of a good style is eternal vigilance.'

10 Variety of 'tone' and 'register' is *not* desirable, where you need 'dignified consistency'. That is explored below on pp. 124–7 of this section.

11 'Naturally' in this instance is a significant pointer rather than a mere interjection, as the main text goes on to argue almost at once.

12 In *both* senses, i.e. 'to understand' and 'to take pleasure in'.

Chapter 6 Making it

1 Yes, we are all familiar with 'horror stories' about sacks of unmarked papers being discovered after results have beeen published, of History papers being sent to Domestic Science teachers or Physics ones to Geographers, of undergraduates being hired because the Boards can't recruit enough trained professionals, and all the rest of it, and I get as concerned about them as anyone else in education, students of course included. But even when corroborated – which is not always the case – they are *exceptions*, however inexcusable, and to walk into an exam hall convinced that you're at the mercy of incompetents is statistically absurd. I'll go further: such a belief is far more stupid than the examiner of your worst nightmares.

2 I am well aware that nowadays that title is as likely to be '*Madam Chief Invigilator*'.

3 The phenomenon has recently been examined by Malcolm Gladwell in his *Blink: The Power of Thinking Without Thinking* (London: Allen Lane, 2005).

Appendix I

1 What is known as 'vanity publishing' is less an exception to this assertion than might appear. Yes, authors determined to get their work in print at any cost have *always* been able to do so; the word *cost*, though, is utterly the point. Private publications – be they worthy or ridiculous – have always been very expensive; as the main text points out in a moment, logging your 'vain' work on the Net is immeasurably cheaper.

2 Two examples might be *De Revolutionibus Orbium Coelestium,* Copernicus's 1547 proof of the nature of our planet and its orbital dependence on the sun, and Salmon Rushdie's 1988 *The Satanic Verses,* which made him an assassination target.

3 Which aren't all that effective, as doubtless you know. The amount of loathsomeness (e.g. inflammatory racism, hard-core porn, religious apocalypticism) the Net offers is something that causes concern right across the political spectrum.

4 That is a remark that some would no doubt find appallingly elitist, but since I'm writing for an elite, so be it.

Bibliography

This is a *highly* selective list, comprising books I admire, have found most valuable, and which I believe will particularly benefit able students. A larger (though still selective) bibliography can be found in my *Studying For Success*.

General

Bill Bryson (1991) *Mother Tongue* Penguin: Harmondsworth.
Tony Buzan (2003) *Use Your Head* BBC: London.
Guy Claxton (2000) *Wise Up: The Challenge of Lifelong Learning* Bloomsbury: London.
Guy Claxton (2005) *The Wayward Mind* Little Brown: London.
William James (1963) *Principles of Psychology* (first published 1890).
C.A. Mace (1969) *The Psychology of Study* Penguin: Harmondsworth.
Richard Palmer (2004) *Studying for Success* Routledge: London.
Jonathan Smith (2000) *The Learning Game* Little Brown: London.
Judith Woolf (2004) *From Notepad to Mousepad* Routledge: London.

Writing

Bill Bryson (1994) *Dictionary For Writers and Editors* Penguin: Harmondsworth.
Sir Ernest Gowers (1987) *The Complete Plain Words* Penguin: Harmondsworth.
John Kirkman (2005) *Full Marks* Routledge: London.
Richard Palmer (2003) *The Good Grammar Guide* Routledge: London.
Richard Palmer (2002) *Write in Style* Routledge: London.

Reading

Manya and Eric De Leeuw (1990) *Read Better, Read Faster* Penguin: Harmondsworth.

Philosophy and practical thinking

Nicholas Alchin (2003) *Theory of Knowledge* John Murray: London.

Simon Blackburn (1999) *Think* Oxford University Press: New York.

Malcolm Gladwell (2005) *Blink: The Power of Thinking Without Thinking* Allen Lane: London.

Ted Honderich (ed.) (2005) *The Oxford Companion to Philosophy* Oxford University Press: Oxford.

John Lechte (1994) *Fifty Key Contemporary Thinkers* Routledge: London.

Roger Trigg (2001) *Philosophy Matters* Blackwell: Oxford.

Nigel Warburton (2000) *Thinking from A to Z* Routledge: London.

Nigel Warburton (2004) *Philosophy: The Basics* Routledge: London.

Frances Wheen (2004) *How Mumbo-Jumbo Conquered the World* Fourth Estate: London.

Index